The Story of Young Abraham Lincoln

Wayne Whipple

Alpha Editions

This edition published in 2024

ISBN : 9789362999702

Design and Setting By
Alpha Editions
www.alphaedis.com
Email - info@alphaedis.com

As per information held with us this book is in Public Domain.
This book is a reproduction of an important historical work. Alpha Editions uses the best technology to reproduce historical work in the same manner it was first published to preserve its original nature. Any marks or number seen are left intentionally to preserve its true form.

Contents

INTRODUCTION .... - 1 -

CHAPTER I .... - 4 -

CHAPTER II .... - 8 -

CHAPTER III .... - 12 -

CHAPTER IV .... - 16 -

CHAPTER V .... - 22 -

CHAPTER VI .... - 27 -

CHAPTER VII .... - 34 -

CHAPTER VIII .... - 42 -

CHAPTER IX .... - 46 -

CHAPTER X .... - 52 -

CHAPTER XI .... - 57 -

CHAPTER XII .... - 64 -

CHAPTER XIII .... - 67 -

CHAPTER XIV .... - 74 -

CHAPTER XV .... - 84 -

CHAPTER XVI ....- 89 -

CHAPTER XVII ....- 96 -

CHAPTER XVIII ....- 99 -

CHAPTER XIX ....- 105 -

CHAPTER XX..- 109 -

CHAPTER XXI ....- 116 -

INTRODUCTION

LINCOLN FROM NEW AND UNUSUAL SOURCES

The boy or girl who reads to-day may know more about the real Lincoln than his own children knew. The greatest President's son, Robert Lincoln, discussing a certain incident in their life in the White House, remarked to the writer, with a smile full of meaning:

"I believe you know more about our family matters than I do!"

This is because "all the world loves a lover"—and Abraham Lincoln loved everybody. With all his brain and brawn, his real greatness was in his heart. He has been called "the Great-Heart of the White House," and there is little doubt that more people have heard about him than there are who have read of the original "Great-Heart" in "The Pilgrim's Progress."

Indeed, it is safe to say that more millions in the modern world are acquainted with the story of the rise of Abraham Lincoln from a poorly built log cabin to the highest place among "the seats of the mighty," than are familiar with the Bible story of Joseph who arose and stood next to the throne of the Pharaohs.

Nearly every year, especially since the Lincoln Centennial, 1909, something new has been added to the universal knowledge of one of the greatest, if not *the* greatest man who ever lived his life in the world. Not only those who "knew Lincoln," but many who only "saw him once" or shook hands with him, have been called upon to tell what they saw him do or heard him say. So hearty was his kindness toward everybody that the most casual remark of his seems to be charged with deep human affection—"the touch of Nature" which has made "the whole world kin" to him.

He knew just how to sympathize with every one. The people felt this, without knowing why, and recognized it in every deed or word or touch, so that those who have once felt the grasp of his great warm hand seem to have been drawn into the strong circuit of "Lincoln fellowship," and were enabled, as if by "the laying on of hands," to speak of him ever after with a deep and tender feeling.

There are many such people who did not rush into print with their observations and experiences. Their Lincoln memories seemed too sacred to scatter far and wide. Some of them have yielded, with real reluctance, in relating all for publication in THE STORY OF YOUNG ABRAHAM LINCOLN only because they wished their recollections to benefit the rising generation.

Several of these modest folk have shed true light on important phases and events in Lincoln's life history. For instance, there has been much discussion concerning Lincoln's Gettysburg Address—where was it written, and did he deliver it from notes?

Now, fifty years after that great occasion, comes a distinguished college professor who unconsciously settles the whole dispute, whether Lincoln held his notes in his right hand or his left—if he used them at all!—while making his immortal "little speech." To a group of veterans of the Grand Army of the Republic he related, casually, what he saw while a college student at Gettysburg, after working his way through the crowd of fifteen thousand people to the front of the platform on that memorable day. From this point of vantage he saw and heard everything, and there is no gainsaying the vivid memories of his first impressions—how the President held the little pages in both hands straight down before him, swinging his tall form to right, to left and to the front again as he emphasized the now familiar closing words, "*of* the people—*by* the people—*for* the people—shall not perish from the earth."

Such data have been gathered from various sources and are here given for the first time in a connected life-story. Several corrections of stories giving rise to popular misconceptions have been supplied by Robert, Lincoln's only living son. One of these is the true version of "Bob's" losing the only copy of his father's first inaugural address. Others were furnished by two aged Illinois friends who were acquainted with "Abe" before he became famous. One of these explained, without knowing it, a question which has puzzled several biographers—how a young man of Lincoln's shrewd intelligence could have been guilty of such a misdemeanor, as captain in the Black Hawk War, as to make it necessary for his superior officer to deprive him of his sword for a single day.

A new story is told by a dear old lady, who did not wish her name given, about herself when she was a little girl, when a "drove of lawyers riding the old Eighth Judicial District of Illinois," came to drink from a famous cold spring on her father's premises. She described the uncouth dress of a tall young man, asking her father who he was, and he replied with a laugh, "Oh, that's Abe Lincoln."

One day in their rounds, as the lawyers came through the front gate, a certain judge, whose name the narrator refused to divulge, knocked down with his cane her pet doll, which was leaning against the fence. The little girl cried over this contemptuous treatment of her "child."

Young Lawyer Lincoln, seeing it all, sprang in and quickly picked up the fallen doll. Brushing off the dust with his great awkward hand he said, soothingly, to the wounded little mother-heart:

"There now, little Black Eyes, don't cry. Your baby's alive. See, she isn't hurt a bit!"

That tall young man never looked uncouth to her after that. It was this same old lady who told the writer that Lawyer Lincoln wore a new suit of clothes for the first time on the very day that he performed the oft-described feat of rescuing a helpless hog from a great deep hole in the road, and plastered his new clothes with mud to the great merriment of his legal friends. This well-known incident occurred not far from her father's place near Paris, Illinois.

These and many other new and corrected incidents are now collected for THE STORY OF YOUNG ABRAHAM LINCOLN, in addition to the best of everything suitable that was known before—as the highest patriotic service which the writer can render to the young people of the United States of America.

WAYNE WHIPPLE.

CHAPTER I

ABRAHAM LINCOLN'S FOREFATHERS

Lincoln's grandfather, for whom he was named Abraham, was a distant cousin to Daniel Boone. The Boones and the Lincolns had intermarried for generations. The Lincolns were of good old English stock. When he was President, Abraham Lincoln, who had never given much attention to the family pedigree, said that the history of his family was well described by a single line in Gray's "Elegy":

"The short and simple annals of the poor."

Yet Grandfather Abraham was wealthy for his day. He accompanied Boone from Virginia to Kentucky and lost his life there. He had sacrificed part of his property to the pioneer spirit within him, and, with the killing of their father, his family lost the rest. They were "land poor" in the wilderness of the "Dark-and-Bloody-Ground"—the meaning of the Indian name, "Ken-tuc-kee."

Grandfather Lincoln had built a solid log cabin and cleared a field or two around it, near the Falls of the Ohio, about where Louisville now stands. But, in the Summer of 1784, the tragic day dawned upon the Lincolns which has come to many a pioneer family in Kentucky and elsewhere. His son Thomas told this story to his children:

HOW INDIANS KILLED "GRANDFATHER LINCOLN"

"My father—your grandfather, Abraham Lincoln—come over the mountains from Virginia with his cousin, Dan'l Boone. He was rich for them times, as he had property worth seventeen thousand dollars; but Mr. Boone he told Father he could make a good deal more by trappin' and tradin' with the Injuns for valuable pelts, or fur skins.

"You know, Dan'l Boone he had lived among the Injuns. He was a sure shot with the rifle so's he could beat the redskins at their own game. They took him a prisoner oncet, and instead of killin' him, they was about ready to make him chief—he pretended all the while as how he'd like that—when he got away from 'em. He was such a good fellow that them Injuns admired his shrewdness, and they let him do about what he pleased. So he thought they'd let Father alone.

"Well, your grandfather was a Quaker, you see, and believed in treatin' them red devils well—like William Penn done, you know. He was a man for peace and quiet, and everything was goin' smooth with the tribes of what we called the Beargrass Country, till one day, when he and my brothers, Mordecai—'Mord' was a big fellow for his age—and Josiah, a few years younger—was out in the clearin' with the oxen, haulin' logs down to the crick. I went along too, but I didn't help much—for I was only six.

"Young as I was, I remember what happened that day like it was only yesterday. It come like a bolt out of the blue. We see Father drop like he was shot—for he *was* shot! Then I heard the crack of a rifle and I saw a puff of smoke floatin' out o' the bushes.

"Injuns!" gasps Mord, and starts on the run for the house—to get his gun. Josiah, he starts right off in the opposite direction to the Beargrass fort—we called it a fort, but it was nothin' but a stockade. The way we boys scattered was like a brood o' young turkeys, or pa'tridges, strikin' for cover when the old one is shot. I knowed I'd ought to run too, but I didn't want to leave my father layin' there on the ground. Seemed like I'd ought to woke him up so he could run too. Yet I didn't feel like touchin' him. I think I must 'a' knowed he was dead.

"While I was standin' still, starin' like the oxen, not knowin' what to do, a big Injun come out o' the brush, with a big knife in his hand. I knowed what he was goin' to do—skelp my father! I braced up to 'im to keep 'im away, an' he jist laffed at me. I never think what the devil looks like without seein' that red demon with his snaky black eyes, grinnin' at me!

TOM LINCOLN CHASED BY INDIANS

"He picked me up like I was a baby an set me on the sawlog, an' was turnin' back to skelp Father, when—biff!—another gun-crack—and Mr. Big Indian he drops jist like your grandfather did, only he wriggles and squirms around, bitin' the dust—like a big snake for all the world!

"I was standin' there, kind o' dazed, watchin' another puff o' white smoke, comin' out between two logs in the side of our house. Then I knowed 'Mord' had shot my Injun. He had run in, got the gun down off'n the wall, an' peekin' out through a crack, he sees that Injun takin' hold o' me. Waitin' till the ol' demon turns away, so's not to hit me, 'Mord' he aims at a silver dangler on Mr. Injun's breast and makes him drop in his tracks like I said. Your Uncle 'Mord' he was a sure shot—like Cousin Dan'l Boone.

"Then I hears the most blood-curdlin' yells, and a lot o' red devils jump out o' the bushes an' come for me brandishin' their tomahawks an' skelpin' knives. It was like hell broke loose. They had been watchin' an', of course, 'twas all right to kill Father, but when 'Mord' killed one o' their bucks, that made a big difference. I had sense enough left to run for the house with them Injuns after me. Seemed like I couldn't run half as fast as usual, but I must 'a' made purty good time, from what 'Mord' an' Mother said afterward.

"He said one was ahead o' the rest an' had his tomahawk raised to brain me with it when—bing!—an' 'Mord' fetches *him* down like he did the fellow that was goin' to skelp Father. That made the others mad an' they took after me, but 'Mord' he drops the head one jist when he's goin' to hit me. But all I knowed at the time was that them red devils was a-chasin' me, and I'd got to 'leg it' for dear life!

"When I gits near enough to the house, I hears Mother and 'Mord' hollerin' to make me run faster and go to the door, for Mother had it open jist wide enough to reach out an' snatch me in—when the third Injun was stoopin' to grab me, but 'Mord' makes him bite the dust like the others.

"My, but wasn't them Injuns mad! Some of 'em sneaked around behind the house—they had to give 'Mord's' gun a wide berth to git there!—but he could only protect the front—and was a-settin' fire to our cabin to smoke us out or roast us alive, jist when the soldiers come with Josiah from the fort and saved our lives. Then the Injuns made 'emselves scurce—but they druv off the oxen and all our other stock.

"MORD" LINCOLN, INDIAN FIGHTER

"That was the breaking up of our family. None of us boys was old enough to take Father's place, an' Mother she was afraid to live there alone. Accordin' to the laws o' Virginia—Kentucky belonged to Virginia then—the oldest son got all the proputty, so 'Mord' he gets it all. He was welcome to it too, for he was the only one of us that could take care of it. 'Mord' he wasn't satisfied with killin' a few Injuns that day to revenge Father's death. He made a business of shootin' 'em on sight—a reg'lar Injun stalker! He couldn't see that he was jist as savage as the worst Injun, to murder 'em without waitin' to see whether Mr. Injun was a friend or a foe.

"Oncet when I told 'im there was good an' bad red men like they wuz good an' bad white men, he said I might jist as well say 'good *devil*' as 'good Injun!' He says 'the only good Injun's the dead Injun!'

"Well, the settlers must 'a' 'greed with 'Mord,' for they made him sheriff o' the county—he was sech a good shot, too—an' they 'lected him to the Legislatur' after Kentucky come in as a State. He stood high in the county. Folks didn't mind his shootin' an' Injun or two, more or less, when he got the chancet. They all looked on redskins like they was catamounts an' other pesky varmints.

"Your grandmother Lincoln an' Josiah an' me moved over into Washington County, but she had hard scrabblin' to git a livin'. Josiah he stayed with her, an' between him an' 'Mord,' they helped her along, but I had to git out and scratch for a livin'. From the time I was ten I was hired out to work for my 'keep,' an' anything else I could git. I knocked aroun' the country, doin' this, that an' t'other thing till I picked up carpenterin' o' Joseph Hanks, a cousin o' mine, an' there I met his sister Nancy, an' that's how she come to be your mother—an' 'bout how I come to be your father, too!"

Little is known today of Mordecai Lincoln, and there would be less interest in poor Thomas if he had not become the father of Abraham Lincoln, the sixteenth President of the United States. Mordecai Lincoln was a joker and humorist. One who knew him well said of him:

"He was a man of great drollery, and it would almost make you laugh to look at him. I never saw but one other man whose quiet, droll look excited in me the disposition to laugh, and that was 'Artemus Ward.'

"Mordecai was quite a story-teller, and in this Abe resembled his 'Uncle Mord,' as we called him. He was an honest man, as tender-hearted as a woman, and to the last degree charitable and benevolent.

"Abe Lincoln had a very high opinion of his uncle, and on one occasion remarked, 'I have often said that Uncle Mord had run off with all the talents of the family.'"

In a letter about his family history, just before he was nominated for the presidency, Abraham Lincoln wrote:

"My parents were both born in Virginia, of undistinguished families—second families, perhaps I should say. My mother was of a family of the name of Hanks. My paternal grandfather, Abraham Lincoln, emigrated from Rockingham County, Virginia, to Kentucky about 1781 or 2, where, a year or two later, he was killed by Indians—not in battle, but by stealth, when he was laboring to open a farm in the forest. His ancestors, who were Quakers, went to Virginia from Berks County, Pennsylvania. An effort to identify them with the New England family of the same name ended in nothing more definite than a similarity of Christian names in both families, such as Enoch, Levi, Mordecai, Solomon, Abraham, and the like.

"My father, at the death of his father, was but six years of age; and he grew up, literally without education."

CHAPTER II

ABRAHAM LINCOLN'S FATHER AND MOTHER

While Thomas Lincoln was living with a farmer and doing odd jobs of carpentering, he met Nancy Hanks, a tall, slender woman, with dark skin, dark brown hair and small, deep-set gray eyes. She had a full forehead, a sharp, angular face and a sad expression. Yet her disposition was generally cheerful. For her backwoods advantages she was considered well educated. She read well and could write, too. It is stated that Nancy Hanks taught Thomas Lincoln to write his own name. Thomas was twenty-eight and Nancy twenty-three when their wedding day came. Christopher Columbus Graham, when almost one hundred years old, gave the following description of the marriage feast of the Lincoln bride and groom:

"I am one of the two living men who can prove that Abraham Lincoln, or Linkhorn, as the family was miscalled, was born in lawful wedlock, for I saw Thomas Lincoln marry Nancy Hanks on the 12th day of June, 1806. I was hunting roots for my medicine and just went to the wedding to get a good supper and got it.

"Tom Lincoln was a carpenter, and a good one for those days, when a cabin was built mainly with the ax, and not a nail or a bolt or hinge in it, only leathers and pins to the doors, and no glass, except in watches and spectacles and bottles. Tom had the best set of tools in what was then and is now Washington County.

"Jesse Head, the good Methodist minister that married them, was also a carpenter or cabinet maker by trade, and as he was then a neighbor, they were good friends.

"While you pin me down to facts, I will say that I saw Nancy Hanks Lincoln at her wedding, a fresh-looking girl, I should say over twenty. Tom was a respectable mechanic and could choose, and she was treated with respect.

"I was at the infare, too, given by John H. Parrott, her guardian, and only girls with money had guardians appointed by the court. We had bear meat; venison; wild turkey and ducks' eggs, wild and tame—so common that you could buy them at two bits a bushel; maple sugar, swung on a string, to bite off for coffee; syrup in big gourds, peach and honey; a sheep that the two families barbecued whole over coals of wood burned in a pit, and covered with green boughs to keep the juices in. Our table was of the puncheons cut from solid logs, and the next day they were the floor of the new cabin."

Thomas Lincoln took his bride to live in a little log cabin in a Kentucky settlement—not a village or hardly a hamlet—called Elizabethtown. He evidently thought this place would be less lonesome for his wife, while he was away hunting and carpentering, than the lonely farm he had purchased in Hardin County, about fourteen miles away. There was so little carpentering or cabinet making to do that he could make a better living by farming or hunting. Thomas was very fond of shooting and as he was a fine marksman he could provide game for the table, and other things which are considered luxuries to-day, such as furs and skins needed for the primitive wearing apparel of the pioneers. A daughter was born to the young couple at Elizabethtown, whom they named Sarah.

Dennis Hanks, a cousin of Nancy, lived near the Lincolns in the early days of their married life, and gave Mrs. Eleanor Atkinson this description of their early life together:

"Looks didn't count them days, nohow. It was stren'th an' work an' daredevil. A lazy man or a coward was jist pizen, an' a spindlin' feller had to stay in the settlemints. The clearin's hadn't no use fur him. Tom was strong, an' he wasn't lazy nor afeer'd o' nothin', but he was kind o' shif'less—couldn't git nothin' ahead, an' didn't keer putickalar. Lots o' them kind o' fellers in 'arly days, 'druther hunt and fish, an' I reckon they had their use. They killed off the varmints an' made it safe fur other fellers to go into the woods with an ax.

"When Nancy married Tom he was workin' in a carpenter shop. It wasn't Tom's fault he couldn't make a livin' by his trade. Thar was sca'cely any money in that kentry. Every man had to do his own tinkerin', an' keep everlastin'ly at work to git enough to eat. So Tom tuk up some land. It was mighty ornery land, but it was the best Tom could git, when he hadn't much to trade fur it.

"Pore? We was all pore, them days, but the Lincolns was porer than anybody. Choppin' trees an' grubbin' roots an' splittin' rails an' huntin' an' trappin' didn't leave Tom no time. It was all he could do to git his fambly enough to eat and to kiver 'em. Nancy was turrible ashamed o' the way they lived, but she knowed Tom was doin' his best, an' she wa'n't the pesterin' kind. She was purty as a pictur' an' smart as you'd find 'em anywhere. She could read an' write. The Hankses was some smarter'n the Lincolns. Tom thought a heap o' Nancy, an' he was as good to her as he knowed how. He didn't drink or swear or play cyards or fight, an' them was drinkin', cussin', quarrelsome days. Tom was popylar, an' he could lick a bully if he had to. He jist couldn't git ahead, somehow."

"NANCY'S BOY BABY"

Evidently Elizabethtown failed to furnish Thomas Lincoln a living wage from carpentering, for he moved with his young wife and his baby girl to a farm on Nolen Creek, fourteen miles away. The chief attraction of the so-called farm was a fine spring of water bubbling up in the shade of a small grove. From this spring the place came to be known as "Rock Spring Farm." It was a barren spot and the cabin on it was a rude and primitive sort of home for a carpenter and joiner to occupy. It contained but a single room, with only one window and one door. There was a wide fireplace in the big chimney which was built outside. But that rude hut became the home of "the greatest American."

Abraham Lincoln was born to poverty and privation, but he was never a pauper. His hardships were those of many other pioneers, the wealthiest of whom suffered greater privations than the poorest laboring man has to endure to-day.

After his nomination to the presidency, Mr. Lincoln gave to Mr. Hicks, a portrait painter, this memorandum of his birth:

"I was born February 12, 1809, in then Hardin County, Kentucky, at a point within the now county of Larue, a mile or a mile and a half from where Hodgen's mill now is. My parents being dead, and my memory not serving, I know no means of identifying the precise locality. It was on Nolen Creek.

"A. LINCOLN.

"JUNE 14, 1860."

The exact spot was identified after his death, and the house was found standing many years later. The logs were removed to Chicago, for the World's Columbian Exposition, in 1893, and the cabin was reconstructed and exhibited there and elsewhere in the United States. The materials were taken back to their original site, and a fine marble structure now encloses the precious relics of the birthplace of "the first American," as Lowell calls Lincoln in his great "Commemoration Ode."

Cousin Dennis Hanks gives the following quaint description of "Nancy's boy baby," as reported by Mrs. Eleanor Atkinson in her little book on "Lincoln's Boyhood."

"Tom an' Nancy lived on a farm about two miles from us, when Abe was born. I ricollect Tom comin' over to our house one cold mornin' in Feb'uary an' sayin' kind o' slow, 'Nancy's got a boy baby.'

"Mother got flustered an' hurried up 'er work to go over to look after the little feller, but I didn't have nothin' to wait fur, so I cut an' run the hull two mile to see my new cousin.

"You bet I was tickled to death. Babies wasn't as common as blackberries in the woods o' Kaintucky. Mother come over an' washed him an' put a yaller flannel petticoat on him, an' cooked some dried berries with wild honey fur Nancy, an' slicked things up an' went home. An' that's all the nuss'n either of 'em got.

"I rolled up in a b'ar skin an' slep' by the fireplace that night, so's I could see the little feller when he cried an' Tom had to get up an' tend to him. Nancy let me hold him purty soon. Folks often ask me if Abe was a good lookin' baby. Well, now, he looked just like any other baby, at fust—like red cherry pulp squeezed dry. An' he didn't improve none as he growed older. Abe never was much fur looks. I ricollect how Tom joked about Abe's long legs when he was toddlin' round the cabin. He growed out o' his clothes faster'n Nancy could make 'em.

"But he was mighty good comp'ny, solemn as a papoose, but interested in everything. An' he always did have fits o' cuttin' up. I've seen him when he was a little feller, settin' on a stool, starin' at a visitor. All of a sudden he'd bu'st out laughin' fit to kill. If he told us what he was laughin' at, half the time we couldn't see no joke.

"Abe never give Nancy no trouble after he could walk excep' to keep him in clothes. Most o' the time he went bar'foot. Ever wear a wet buckskin glove? Them moccasins wasn't no putection ag'inst the wet. Birch bark with hickory bark soles, strapped on over yarn socks, beat buckskin all holler, fur snow. Abe'n me got purty handy contrivin' things that way. An' Abe was right out in the woods about as soon's he was weaned, fishin' in the creek, settin' traps fur rabbits an' muskrats, goin' on coon-hunts with Tom an' me an' the dogs, follerin' up bees to find bee-trees, an' drappin' corn fur his pappy. Mighty interestin' life fur a boy, but thar was a good many chances he wouldn't live to grow up."

When little Abe was four years old his father and mother moved from Rock Spring Farm to a better place on Knob Creek, a few miles to the northeast of the farm where he was born.

CHAPTER III

THE BOY LINCOLN'S BEST TEACHER

At Knob Creek the boy began to go to an "A B C" school. His first teacher was Zachariah Riney. Of course, there were no regular schools in the backwoods then. When a man who "knew enough" happened to come along, especially if he had nothing else to do, he tried to teach the children of the pioneers in a poor log schoolhouse. It is not likely that little Abe went to school more than a few weeks at this time, for he never had a year's schooling in his life. There was another teacher afterward at Knob Creek—a man named Caleb Hazel. Little is known of either of these teachers except that he taught little Abe Lincoln. If their pupil had not become famous the men and their schools would never have been mentioned in history.

An old man, named Austin Gollaher, used to like to tell of the days when he and little Abe went to school together. He said:

"Abe was an unusually bright boy at school, and made splendid progress in his studies. Indeed, he learned faster than any of his schoolmates. Though so young, he studied very hard."

Although Nancy Lincoln insisted on sending the children to school, when there was any, she had a large share in Abe's early education, just as she had taught his father to write his own name. She told them Bible stories and such others as she had picked up in her barren, backwoods life. She and her husband were too religious to believe in telling their children fairy tales.

The best thing of all was the reading of "The Pilgrim's Progress" during the long Winter evenings, after the wood was brought in and Father Tom had set his traps and done his other work for the night. Nancy's voice was low, with soft, southern tones and accents. Tom and the children enjoyed the story of Christian's pilgrimage from the City of Destruction to the Celestial City the more because of her love for the story she was reading to them, as they lay on bearskin rugs before the blazing fire.

Abe was only six, but he was a thoughtful boy. He tried to think of some way to show his gratitude to his mother for giving them so much pleasure. While out gathering sticks and cutting wood for the big fireplace, a happy thought came to him—he would cut off some spicewood branches, hack them up on a log, and secrete them behind the cabin. Then, when the mother was ready to read again, and Sarah and the father were sitting and lying before the fire, he brought in the hidden branches and threw them on, a few twigs at a time, to the surprise of the others. It worked like a charm; the spicewood boughs not only added to the brightness of the scene but filled the whole house with the "sweet smelling savour" of a little boy's love and gratitude.

No one can fathom the pleasure of that precious memory throughout those four lives, as the story of Great Heart and Christiana followed Christian along the path that "shineth more and more unto the perfect day." While the father and sister were delighted with the crackle, sparkle and pleasant aroma of the bits of spicewood, as Abe tossed them upon the fire, no one could appreciate the thoughtful act of the boy so much as his mother. It would be strange if her eyes did not fill, as she read to her fascinated family, but that was not the sort of thing the fondest mother could speak of.

Little did Nancy dream that, in reading to her son of the devotion of Great Heart to his charges, she was fostering a spirit in her little son that would help him make the noble pilgrimage from their hovel to the highest home in the land, where another President of the United States would refer to him as "the Great Heart of the White House." If any one could have looked ahead fifty years to see all this, and could have told Nancy Hanks Lincoln, she would not have believed it. After her own life of toil and hardship it would have seemed to her "too good to be true." But in the centuries following the humble yet beautiful career of "the Backwoods Boy" from the hut to the White House, history keeps the whole world saying with bated breath, "the half was never told!"

AN OLD MAN'S STORY OF SAVING ABRAHAM LINCOLN'S LIFE

Austin Gollaher, grown to manhood, still living in his old log cabin near the Lincoln house in Knob Creek nearly twenty years after Lincoln's assassination, and gave the following account of an adventure he had with the little Lincoln boy:

"I once saved Lincoln's life. We had been going to school together one year; but the next year we had no school, because there were so few scholars to attend, there being only about twenty in the school the year before.

"Consequently Abe and I had not much to do; but, as we did not go to school and our mothers were strict with us, we did not get to see each other very often. One Sunday morning my mother waked me up early, saying she was going to see Mrs. Lincoln, and that I could go along. Glad of the chance, I was soon dressed and ready to go. After my mother and I got there, Abe and I played all through the day.

"While we were wandering up and down the little stream called Knob Creek, Abe said: 'Right up there'—pointing to the east—'we saw a covey of partridges yesterday. Let's go over.' The stream was too wide for us to jump across. Finally we saw a foot-log, and decided to try it. It was narrow, but Abe said, 'Let's coon it.'

"I went first and reached the other side all right. Abe went about half way across, when he got scared and began trembling. I hollered to him, 'Don't look down nor up nor sideways, but look right at me and hold on tight!' But he fell off into the creek, and, as the water was about seven or eight feet deep (I could not swim, and neither could Abe), I knew it would do no good for me to go in after him.

"So I got a stick—a long water sprout—and held it out to him. He came up, grabbing with both hands, and I put the stick into his hands. He clung to it, and I pulled him out on the bank, almost dead. I got him by the arms and shook him well, and then I rolled him on the ground, when the water poured out of his mouth.

"He was all right very soon. We promised each other that we would never tell anybody about it, and never did for years. I never told any one of it till after Lincoln was killed."

Abraham Lincoln's parents were religious in their simple way. The boy was brought up to believe in the care of the Father in Heaven over the affairs of this life. The family attended camp meetings and preaching services, which were great events, because few and far between, in those primitive days. Abe used afterward to get his playmates together and preach to them in a way that sometimes frightened them and made them cry.

No doubt young Lincoln learned more that was useful to him in after life from the wandering preachers of his day than he did of his teachers during the few months that he was permitted to go to school. But his best teacher was his mother. She would have been proud to have her boy grow up to be a traveling minister or exhorter, like Peter Cartwright, "the backwoods preacher."

Nancy Hanks Lincoln "builded better than she knew." She would have been satisfied with a cabin life for her son. She little knew that by her own life and teaching she was raising up the greatest man of his age, and one of the grandest men in all history, to become the ruler of the greatest nation that the world has ever seen. She did her duty by her little boy and he honored her always during her life and afterward. No wonder he once exclaimed when he thought of her:

"All I am or hope to be I owe to my sainted mother."

And out of her poor, humble life, that devoted woman

"Gave us Lincoln and never knew!"

CHAPTER IV

LEARNING TO WORK

The little Lincoln boy learned to help his father and mother as soon as he could, picking berries, dropping seeds and carrying water for the men to drink. The farm at Knob Creek seems to have been a little more fertile than the other two places on which his father had chosen to live.

Once while living in the White House, President Lincoln was asked if he could remember his "old Kentucky home." He replied with considerable feeling:

"I remember that old home very well. Our farm was composed of three fields. It lay in the valley, surrounded by high hills and deep gorges. Sometimes, when there came a big rain in the hills, the water would come down through the gorges and spread all over the farm. The last thing I remember of doing there was one Saturday afternoon; the other boys planted the corn in what we called the big field—it contained seven acres—and I dropped the pumpkin seed. I dropped two seeds in every other row and every other hill. The next Sunday morning there came a big rain in the hills—it did not rain a drop in the valley, but the water, coming through the gorges, washed the ground, corn, pumpkin seeds and all, clear off the field!"

Although this was the last thing Lincoln could remember doing on that farm, it is not at all likely that it was the last thing he did there, for Thomas Lincoln was not the man to plant corn in a field he was about to leave. (The Lincolns moved away in the fall.)

Another baby boy was born at Knob Creek farm; a puny, pathetic little stranger. When this baby was about three years old, the father had to use his skill as a cabinet maker in making a tiny coffin, and the Lincoln family wept over a lonely little grave in the wilderness.

About this time Abe began to learn lessons in practical patriotism. Once when Mr. Lincoln was asked what he could remember of the War of 1812, he replied:

"Nothing but this: I had been fishing one day and caught a little fish which I was taking home. I met a soldier on the road, and, having been told at home that we must be good to the soldiers, I gave him my fish."

An old man, Major Alexander Sympson, who lived not far from the Lincolns at this period, left this description of "a mere spindle of a boy," in one of his earliest attempts to defend himself against odds, while waiting at the neighboring mill while a grist was being ground.

"He was the shyest, most reticent, most uncouth and awkward-appearing, homeliest and worst-dressed of any in the crowd. So superlatively wretched a butt could not hope to look on long unmolested. He was attacked one day as he stood near a tree by a larger boy with others at his back. But the crowd was greatly astonished when little Lincoln soundly thrashed the first, the second, and third boy in succession; and then, placing his back against the tree, he defied the whole crowd, and told them they were a lot of cowards."

Evidently Father Tom, who enjoyed quite a reputation as a wrestler, had give the small boy a few lessons in "the manly art of self-defense."

Meanwhile the little brother and sister were learning still better things at their mother's knee, alternately hearing and reading stories from the Bible, "The Pilgrim's Progress," "Æsop's Fables," "Robinson Crusoe," and other books, common now, but rare enough in the backwoods in those days.

There were hard times, even in the wilderness of Kentucky, after the War of 1812. Slavery was spreading, and Thomas and Nancy Lincoln heartily hated that "relic of barbarism." To avoid witnessing its wrongs which made it harder for self-respecting white men to rise above the class referred to with contempt in the South as "poor white trash," Tom Lincoln determined to move farther north and west—and deeper into the wilds.

It is sometimes stated that Abraham Lincoln belonged to the indolent class known as "poor whites," but this is not true. Shiftless and improvident though his father was, he had no use for that class of white slaves, who seemed to fall even lower than the blacks.

There was trouble, too, about the title to much of the land in Kentucky, while Indiana offered special inducements to settlers in that new territory.

In his carpenter work, Thomas Lincoln had learned how to build a flatboat, and had made at least one trip to New Orleans on a craft which he himself had put together. So, when he finally decided in the fall of 1816 to emigrate to Indiana, he at once began to build another boat, which he launched on the Rolling Fork, at the mouth of Knob Creek, about half a mile from his own cabin. He traded his farm for what movable property he could get, and loaded his raft with that and his carpenter tools. Waving good-bye to his wife and two children, he floated down the Rolling Fork, Salt River, and out into the Ohio River, which proved too rough for his shaky craft, and it soon went to pieces.

After fishing up the carpenter tools and most of his other effects, he put together a crazy raft which held till he landed at Thompson's Ferry, Perry County, in Southern Indiana. Here he unloaded his raft, left his valuables in the care of a settler named Posey and journeyed on foot through the woods to find a good location. After trudging about sixteen miles, blazing a trail, he found a situation which suited him well enough, he thought. Then he walked all the way back to the Kentucky home they were about to leave.

He found his wife, with Sarah, aged nine, and Abraham, aged seven, ready to migrate with him to a newer wilderness. The last thing Nancy Lincoln had done before leaving their old home was to take the brother and sister for a farewell visit to the grave of "the little boy that died."

OVER IN INDIANA

The place the father had selected for their home was a beautiful spot. They could build their cabin on a little hill, sloping gently down on all sides. The soil was excellent, but there was one serious drawback—there was no water fit to drink within a mile! Thomas Lincoln had neglected to observe this most important point while he was prospecting. His wife, or even little Abe, would have had more common sense. That was one reason why Thomas Lincoln, though a good man, who tried hard enough at times, was always poor and looked down upon by his thrifty neighbors.

Instead of taking his wife and children down the three streams by boat, as he had gone, the father borrowed two horses of a neighbor and "packed through to Posey's," where he had left his carpenter tools and the other property he had saved from the wreck of his raft. Abe and Sarah must have enjoyed the journey, especially camping out every night on the way. The father's skill as a marksman furnished them with tempting suppers and breakfasts of wild game.

On the horses they packed their bedding and the cooking utensils they needed while on the journey, and for use after their arrival at the new home. This stock was not large, for it consisted only of "one oven and lid, one skillet and lid, and some tinware."

After they came to Posey's, Thomas Lincoln hired a wagon and loaded it with the effects he had left there, as well as the bedding and the cooking things they had brought with them on the two horses. It was a rough wagon ride, jolting over stumps, logs, and roots of trees. An earlier settler had cut out a path for a few miles, but the rest of the way required many days, for the father had to cut down trees to make a rough road wide enough for the wagon to pass. It is not likely that Abe and Sarah minded the delays, for children generally enjoy new experiences of that sort. As for their mother, she was accustomed to all such hardships; she had learned to take life as it came and make the best of it.

Nancy Lincoln needed all her Christian fortitude in that Indiana home—if such a place could be called a home. At last they reached the chosen place, in the "fork" made by Little Pigeon Creek emptying into Big Pigeon Creek, about a mile and a half from a settlement which was afterward called Gentryville.

As it was late in the fall, Thomas Lincoln decided not to wait to cut down big trees and hew logs for a cabin, so he built a "half-faced camp," or shed enclosed on three sides, for his family to live in that winter. As this shed was made of saplings and poles, he put an ax in Abe's hands, and the seven-year-old boy helped his father build their first "home" in Indiana. It was Abe's first experience in the work that afterward made him famous as "the rail splitter." It was with the ax, as it were, that he hewed his way to the White House and became President of the United States.

Of course, little Abe Lincoln had no idea of the White House then. He may never have heard of "the President's Palace," as it used to be called—for the White House was then a gruesome, blackened ruin, burned by the British in the War of 1812. President Madison was living in a rented house nearby, while the Executive Mansion was being restored. The blackened stone walls, left standing after the fire, were *painted white*, and on that account the President's mansion came to be known as "the White House."

Little Abe, without a thought of his great future, was getting ready for it by hacking away at poles and little trees and helping his father in the very best way he knew. It was not long, then, before the "half-faced camp" was ready for his mother and sister to move into.

Then there was the water question. Dennis Hanks afterward said: "Tom Lincoln riddled his land like a honeycomb" trying to find good water. In the fall and winter they caught rainwater or melted snow and strained it, but that was not very healthful at best. So Abe and Sarah had to go a mile to a spring and carry all the water they needed to drink, and, when there had been no rain for a long time, all the water they used for cooking and washing had to be brought from there, too.

When warmer weather came, after their "long and dreary winter" of shivering in that poor shed, the "camp" did not seem so bad. Thomas Lincoln soon set about building a warmer and more substantial cabin. Abe was now eight years old, and had had some practice in the use of the ax, so he was able to help his father still more by cutting and hewing larger logs for the new cabin. They got it ready for the family to move into before cold weather set in again.

They had to make their own furniture also. The table and chairs were made of "puncheon," or slabs of wood, with holes bored under each corner to stick the legs in. Their bedsteads were poles fitted into holes bored in logs in the walls of the cabin, and the protruding ends supported by poles or stakes driven into the ground, for Tom Lincoln had not yet laid the puncheon floor of their cabin. Abe's bed was a pile of dry leaves laid in one corner of the loft to which he climbed by means of a ladder of pegs driven into the wall, instead of stairs.

Their surroundings were such as to delight the heart of a couple of carefree children. The forest was filled with oaks, beeches, walnuts and sugar-maple trees, growing close together and free from underbrush. Now and then there was an open glade called a prairie or "lick," where the wild animals came to drink and disport themselves. Game was plentiful—deer, bears, pheasants, wild turkeys, ducks and birds of all kinds. This, with Tom Lincoln's passion for hunting, promised good things for the family to eat, as well as bearskin rugs for the bare earth floor, and deerskin curtains for the still open door and window. There were fish in the streams and wild fruits and nuts of many kinds to be found in the woods during the summer and fall. For a long time the corn for the "corndodgers" which they baked in the ashes, had to be ground by pounding, or in primitive hand-mills. Potatoes were about the only vegetable raised in large quantities, and pioneer families often made the whole meal of roasted potatoes. Once when his father had "asked the blessing" over an ashy heap of this staple, Abe remarked that they were "mighty poor blessings!"

But there were few complaints. They were all accustomed to that way of living, and they enjoyed the free and easy life of the forest. Their only reason for complaint was because they had been compelled to live in an open shed all winter, and because there was no floor to cover the damp ground in their new cabin—no oiled paper for their one window, and no door swinging in the single doorway—yet the father was carpenter and cabinet maker! There is no record that Nancy Lincoln, weak and ailing though she was, demurred even at such needless privations.

About the only reference to this period of their life that has been preserved for us was in an odd little sketch in which Mr. Lincoln wrote of himself as "he."

"A few days before the completion of his eighth year, in the absence of his father, a flock of wild turkeys approached the new log cabin, and Abraham, with a rifle gun, standing inside, shot through a crack and killed one of them. He has never since pulled a trigger on any larger game."

Though shooting was the principal sport of the youth and their fathers in Lincoln's younger days, Abe was too kind to inflict needless suffering upon any of God's creatures. He had real religion in his loving heart. Even as a boy he seemed to know that

"He prayeth best who loveth best
All things both great and small;
For the dear God that loveth us,
He made and loveth all."

CHAPTER V

LOSING HIS MOTHER

In the fall of 1817, when the Lincoln family had moved from the shed into the rough log cabin, Thomas and Betsy Sparrow came and occupied the "darned little half-faced camp," as Dennis Hanks called it. Betsy Sparrow was the aunt who had brought up Nancy Hanks, and she was now a foster-mother to Dennis, her nephew. Dennis became the constant companion of the two Lincoln children. He has told most of the stories that are known of this sad time in the Lincoln boy's life.

The two families had lived there for nearly a year when Thomas and Betsy Sparrow were both seized with a terrible disease known to the settlers as the "milk-sick" because it attacked the cattle. The stricken uncle and aunt died, early in October, within a few days of each other. While his wife was ill with the same dread disease, Thomas Lincoln was at work, cutting down trees and ripping boards out of the logs with a long whipsaw with a handle at each end, which little Abe had to help him use. It was a sorrowful task for the young lad, for Abe must have known that he would soon be helping his father make his mother's coffin. They buried the Sparrows under the trees "without benefit of clergy," for ministers came seldom to that remote region.

Nancy Lincoln did not long survive the devoted aunt and uncle. She had suffered too much from exposure and privation to recover her strength when she was seized by the strange malady. One who was near her during her last illness wrote, long afterward:

"She struggled on, day by day, like the patient Christian woman she was. Abe and his sister Sarah waited on their mother, and did the little jobs and errands required of them. There was no physician nearer than thirty-five miles.

"The mother knew that she was going to die, and called the children to her bedside. She was very weak and the boy and girl leaned over her while she gave them her dying message. Placing her feeble hand on little Abe's head, she told him to be kind and good to his father and sister.

"'Be good to one another,' she said to them both. While expressing her hope that they might live, as she had taught them to live, in the love of their kindred and the service of God, Nancy Hanks Lincoln passed from the miserable surroundings of her poor life on earth to the brightness of the Beyond, on the seventh day after she was taken sick."

To the motherless boy the thought of his blessed mother being buried without any religious service whatever added a keen pang to the bitterness of his lot. Dennis Hanks once told how eagerly Abe learned to write:

"Sometimes he would write with a piece of charcoal, or the p'int of a burnt stick, on the fence or floor. We got a little paper at the country town, and I made ink out of blackberry juice, briar root and a little copperas in it. It was black, but the copperas would eat the paper after a while. I made his first pen out of a turkey-buzzard feather. We hadn't no geese them days—to make good pens of goose quills."

As soon as he was able Abe Lincoln wrote his first letter. It was addressed to Parson Elkin, the Baptist preacher, who had sometimes stayed over night with the family when they lived in Kentucky, to ask that elder to come and preach a sermon over his mother's grave. It had been a long struggle to learn to write "good enough for a preacher"—especially for a small boy who is asking such a favor of a man as "high and mighty" as a minister of the Gospel seemed to him.

It was a heartbroken plea, but the lad did not realize it. It was a short, straightforward note, but the good preacher's eyes filled with tears as he read it.

The great undertaking was not finished when the letter was written. The postage was a large matter for a little boy. It cost sixpence (equal to twelve-and-a-half cents today) to send a letter a short distance—up to thirty miles. Some letters required twenty-five cents—equal to fifty in modern money. Sometimes, when the sender could not advance the postage, the receiver had to pay it before the letter could be opened and read. On this account letters were almost as rare and as expensive as telegrams are today. When the person getting a letter could not pay the postage, it was returned to the writer, who had to pay double to get it back.

In those days one person could annoy another and put him to expense by writing him and forcing him to pay the postage—then when the letter was opened, it was found to be full of abuse, thus making a man pay for insults to himself!

There was a great general who had suffered in this way, so he made a rule that he would receive no letters unless the postage was prepaid. One day there came to his address a long envelope containing what seemed to be an important document. But it was not stamped, and the servant had been instructed not to receive that kind of mail. So it was returned to the sender. When it came back it was discovered that it had been mailed by mistake without a stamp. That letter announced to General Zachary Taylor that he had been nominated by a great convention as candidate for President of the United States!

All this seems very strange now that a letter can be sent around the world for a few cents. Besides, the mails did not go often and were carried on horseback. For a long time one half-sick old man carried the mail on a good-for-nothing horse, once a week, between New York and Philadelphia, though they were the largest cities in the country.

So it was many months before Abe received an answer to his letter. Elder Elkin may have been away from home on one of the long circuits covered by pioneer preachers. As the days and weeks went by without the lad's receiving any reply he was filled with misgivings lest he had imposed upon the good man's former friendship.

At last the answer came and poor Abe's anxiety was turned to joy. The kind elder not only said he would come, but he also named the Sunday when it would be, so that the Lincoln family could invite all their friends from far and near to the postponed service—for it often happened in this new country that the funeral could not take place for months after the burial.

It was late in the following Summer, nearly a year after Nancy's death, that the devoted minister came. The word had gone out to all the region round about. It was the religious event of the season. Hundreds of people of all ages came from twenty miles around on horseback—a father, mother and two children on one horse—also in oxcarts, and on foot. They sat in groups in the wagons, and on the green grass, as at the feeding of the multitudes in the time of the Christ. But these people brought their own refreshments as if it were a picnic.

They talked together in low, solemn tones while waiting for the poor little funeral procession to march out from the Lincoln cabin to the grass-covered grave. Pioneer etiquette required the formalities of a funeral. Elder Elkin was followed by the widowed husband, with Abraham and Sarah and poor Cousin Dennis, also bereaved of his foster-parents, and now a member of the Lincoln family.

There were tender hearts behind those hardened faces, and tears glistened on the tanned cheeks of many in that motley assemblage of eager listeners, while the good elder was paying the last tribute of earth to the sweet and patient memory of his departed friend of other days.

The words of the man of God, telling that assembled multitude what a lovely and devoted girl and woman his mother had been, gave sweet and solemn joy to the soul of the little Lincoln boy. It was all for her dear sake, and she was, of all women, worthy of this sacred respect. As he gazed around on the weeping people, he thought of the hopes and fears of the months that had passed since he wrote his first letter to bring this about.

"God bless my angel mother!" burst from his lonely lips—"how glad I am I've learned to write!"

THE COMING OF ANOTHER MOTHER

All that a young girl of twelve could do, assisted by a willing brother of ten, was done by Sarah and Abraham Lincoln to make that desolate cabin a home for their lonesome father, and for cousin Dennis Hanks, whose young life had been twice darkened by a double bereavement. But "what is home without a mother?" Thomas Lincoln, missing the balance and inspiration of a patient wife, became more and more restless, and, after a year, wandered back again to his former homes and haunts in Kentucky.

While visiting Elizabethtown he saw a former sweetheart, the Sally Bush of younger days, now Mrs. Daniel Johnston, widow of the county jailer who had recently died, leaving three children and considerable property, for that time and place. Thomas renewed his suit and won the pitying heart of Sarah Johnston, and according to the story of the county clerk:

"The next morning, December 2, 1819, I issued the license, and the same day they were married, bundled up, and started for home."

Imagine the glad surprise of the three children who had been left at home for weeks, when they saw a smart, covered wagon, drawn by four horses, driven up before the cabin door one bright winter day, and their father, active and alert, spring out and assist a pleasant-looking woman and three children to alight! Then they were told that this woman was to be their mother and they had two more sisters and another brother!

To the poor forlorn Lincoln children and their still more desolate cousin, it seemed too good to be true. They quickly learned the names of their new brother and sisters. The Johnston children were called John, Sarah and Matilda, so Sarah Lincoln's name was promptly changed to Nancy for her dead mother, as there were two Sarahs already in the combined family.

Mrs. Sarah Bush Johnston Lincoln lost no time in taking poor Abe and Nancy Lincoln to her great motherly heart, as if they were her own. They were dirty, for they had been neglected, ill-used and deserted. She washed their wasted bodies clean and dressed them in nice warm clothing provided for her own children, till she, as she expressed it, "made them look more human."

Dennis Hanks told afterward of the great difference the stepmother made in their young lives:

"In fact, in a few weeks all had changed; and where everything had been wanting, all was snug and comfortable. She was a woman of great energy, of remarkable good sense, very industrious and saving, also very neat and tidy in her person and manners. She took an especial liking for young Abe. Her love for him was warmly returned, and continued to the day of his death. But few children love their parents as he loved his stepmother. She dressed him up in entire new clothes, and from that time on he appeared to lead a new life. He was encouraged by her to study, and a wish on his part was gratified when it could be done. The two sets of children got along finely together, as if they all had been the children of the same parents."

Dennis also referred to the "large supply of household goods" the new mother brought with her:

"One fine bureau (worth $40), one table, one set of chairs, one large clothes chest, cooking utensils, knives, forks, bedding and other articles."

It must have been a glorious day when such a splendid array of household furniture was carried into the rude cabin of Thomas Lincoln. But best of all, the new wife had sufficient tact and force of will to induce her good-hearted but shiftless husband to lay a floor, put in a window, and hang a door to protect his doubled family from the cold. It was about Christmas time, and the Lincoln children, as they nestled in warm beds for the first time in their lives, must have thanked their second mother from the bottoms of their grateful hearts.

CHAPTER VI

SCHOOL DAYS NOW AND THEN

Lincoln once wrote, in a letter to a friend, about his early teachers in Indiana:

"He (father) removed from Kentucky to what is now Spencer County, Indiana, in my eighth year. We reached our new home about the time the State came into the Union. It was a wild region with many bears and other wild animals still in the woods. There I grew up. There were some schools, so-called; but no qualification was ever required of a teacher beside readin', writin', and cipherin' to the Rule of Three (simple proportion). If a straggler supposed to understand Latin happened to sojourn in the neighborhood, he was looked upon as a wizard. There was absolutely nothing to excite ambition for education."

Abe's first teacher in Indiana, however, was Hazel Dorsey. The school house was built of rough, round logs. The chimney was made of poles well covered with clay. The windows were spaces cut in the logs, and covered with greased paper. But Abe was determined to learn. He and his sister thought nothing of walking four miles a day through snow, rain and mud. "Nat" Grigsby, who afterward married the sister, spoke in glowing terms of Abe's few school days:

"He was always at school early, and attended to his studies. He lost no time at home, and when not at work was at his books. He kept up his studies on Sunday, and carried his books with him to work, so that he might read when he rested from labor."

Thomas Lincoln had no use for "eddication," as he called it. "It will spile the boy," he kept saying. He—the father—had got along better without going to school, and why should Abe have a better education than his father? He thought Abe's studious habits were due to "pure laziness, jest to git shet o' workin'." So, whenever there was the slightest excuse, he took Abe out of school and set him to work at home or for one of the neighbors, while he himself went hunting or loafed about the house.

This must have been very trying to a boy as hungry to learn as Abe Lincoln was. His new mother saw and sympathized with him, and in her quiet way, managed to get the boy started to school, for a few weeks at most. For some reason Hazel Dorsey stopped "keeping" the school, and there was a long "vacation" for all the children. But a new man, Andrew

Crawford, came and settled near Gentryville. Having nothing better to do at first, he was urged to reopen the school.

One evening Abe came in from his work and his stepmother greeted him with:

"Another chance for you to go to school."

"Where?"

"That man Crawford that moved in a while ago is to begin school next week, and two miles and back every day will be just about enough for you to walk to keep your legs limber."

The tactful wife accomplished it somehow and Abe started off to school with Nancy, and a light heart. A neighbor described him as he appeared in Crawford's school, as "long, wiry and strong, while his big feet and hands, and the length of his legs and arms, were out of all proportion to his small trunk and head. His complexion was swarthy, and his skin shriveled and yellow even then. He wore low shoes, buckskin breeches, linsey-woolsey shirt, and a coonskin cap. The breeches hung close to his legs, but were far from meeting the tops of his shoes, exposing 'twelve inches of shinbone, sharp, blue and narrow.'"

"Yet," said Nat Grigsby, "he was always in good health, never sick, and had an excellent constitution."

HELPING KATE ROBY SPELL

Andrew Crawford must have been an unusual man, for he tried to teach "manners" in his backwoods school! Spelling was considered a great accomplishment. Abe shone as a speller in school and at the spelling-matches. One day, evidently during a period when young Lincoln was kept from school to do some outside work for his father, he appeared at the window when the class in spelling was on the floor. The word "defied" was given out and several pupils had misspelled it. Kate Roby, the pretty girl of the village, was stammering over it. "D-e-f," said Kate, then she hesitated over the next letter. Abe pointed to his eye and winked significantly. The girl took the hint and went on glibly "i-e-d," and "went up head."

"I DID IT!"

There was a buck's head nailed over the school house door. It proved a temptation to young Lincoln, who was tall enough to reach it easily. One day the schoolmaster discovered that one horn was broken and he demanded to know who had done the damage. There was silence and a general denial till Abe spoke up sturdily:

"I did it. I did not mean to do it, but I hung on it—and it broke!" The other boys thought Abe was foolish to "own up" till he had to—but that was his way.

It is doubtful if Abe Lincoln owned an arithmetic. He had a copybook, made by himself, in which he entered tables of weights and measures and "sums" he had to do. Among these was a specimen of schoolboy doggerel:

"Abraham Lincoln,
His hand and pen,
He will be good—
But God knows when!"

In another place he wrote some solemn reflections on the value of time:

"Time, what an empty vapor 'tis,
And days, how swift they are!
Swift as an Indian arrow—
Fly on like a shooting star.
The present moment, just, is here,
Then slides away in haste,
That we can never say they're ours,
But only say they're past."

As he grew older his handwriting improved and he was often asked to "set copies" for other boys to follow. In the book of a boy named Richardson, he wrote this prophetic couplet:

"Good boys who to their books apply
Will all be great men by and by."

A "MOTHER'S BOY"—HIS FOOD AND CLOTHING

Dennis Hanks related of his young companion: "As far as food and clothing were concerned, the boy had plenty—such as it was—'corndodgers,' bacon and game, some fish and wild fruits. We had very little wheat flour. The nearest mill was eighteen miles. A hoss mill it was, with a plug (old horse) pullin' a beam around; and Abe used to say his dog could stand and eat the flour as fast as it was made, *and then be ready for supper!*

"For clothing he had jeans. He was grown before he wore all-wool pants. It was a new country, and he was a raw boy, rather a bright and likely lad; but the big world seemed far ahead of him. We were all slow-goin' folks. But he had the stuff of greatness in him. He got his rare sense and sterling principles from both parents. But Abe's kindliness, humor, love of humanity, hatred of slavery, all came from his mother. I am free to say Abe was a 'mother's boy.'"

Dennis used to like to tell of Abe's earliest ventures in the fields of literature: "His first readin' book was Webster's speller. Then he got hold of a book—I can't rickilect the name. It told about a feller, a nigger or suthin', that sailed a flatboat up to a rock, and the rock was magnetized and drawed the nails out of his boat, an' he got a duckin', or drownded, or suthin', I forget now. (This book, of course, was 'The Arabian Nights.') Abe would lay on the floor with a chair under his head, and laugh over them stories by the hour. I told him they was likely lies from end to end; but he learned to read right well in them."

His stock of books was small, but they were the right kind—the Bible, "The Pilgrim's Progress," Æsop's Fables, "Robinson Crusoe," a history of the United States, and the Statutes of Indiana. This last was a strange book for a boy to read, but Abe pored over it as eagerly as a lad to-day might read "The Three Guardsmen," or "The Hound of the Baskervilles." He made notes of what he read with his turkey-buzzard pen and brier-root ink. If he did not have these handy, he would write with a piece of charcoal or the charred end of a stick, on a board, or on the under side of a chair or bench. He used the wooden fire shovel for a slate, shaving it off clean when both sides were full of figures. When he got hold of paper enough to make a copy-book he would go about transferring his notes from boards, beams, under sides of the chairs and the table, and from all the queer places he had put them down, on the spur of the moment.

Besides the books he had at hand, he borrowed all he could get, often walking many miles for a book, until, as he once told a friend, he "read through every book he had ever heard of in that country, for a circuit of fifty miles"—quite a circulating library!

"THE BEGINNING OF LOVE"

"The thoughts of youth are long, long thoughts." It must have been about this time that the lad had the following experience, which he himself related to a legal friend, with his chair tilted back and his knees "cocked up" in the manner described by Cousin John Hanks:

"Did you ever write out a story in your mind? I did when I was little codger. One day a wagon with a lady and two girls and a man broke down near us, and while they were fixing up, they cooked in our kitchen. The woman had books and read us stories, and they were the first of the kind I ever heard. I took a great fancy to one of the girls; and when they were gone I thought of her a good deal, and one day, when I was sitting out in the sun by the house, I wrote out a story in my mind.

"I thought I took my father's horse and followed the wagon, and finally I found it, and they were surprised to see me.

"I talked with the girl and persuaded her to elope with me; and that night I put her on my horse and we started off across the prairie. After several hours we came to a camp; and when we rode up we found it was one we had left a few hours before and went in.

"The next night we tried again, and the same thing happened—the horse came back to the same place; and then we concluded we ought not to elope. I stayed until I had persuaded her father that he ought to give her to me.

"I always meant to write that story out and publish it, and I began once; but I concluded it was not much of a story.

"But I think that was the beginning of love with me."

HOW ABE CAME TO OWN WEEMS'S "LIFE OF WASHINGTON"

Abe's chief delight, if permitted to do so, was to lie in the shade of some inviting tree and read. He liked to lie on his stomach before the fire at night, and often read as long as this flickering light lasted. He sometimes took a book to bed to read as soon as the morning light began to come through the chinks between the logs beside his bed. He once placed a book between the logs to have it handy in the morning, and a storm came up and soaked it with dirty water from the "mud-daubed" mortar, plastered between the logs of the cabin.

The book happened to be Weems's "Life of Washington." Abe was in a sad dilemma. What could he say to the owner of the book, which he had borrowed from the meanest man in the neighborhood, Josiah Crawford, who was so unpopular that he went by the nickname of "Old Blue Nose"?

The only course was to show the angry owner his precious volume, warped and stained as it was, and offer to do anything he could to repay him.

"Abe," said "Old Blue Nose," with bloodcurdling friendliness, "bein' as it's you, Abe, I won't be hard on you. You jest come over and pull fodder for me, and the book is yours."

"All right," said Abe, his deep-set eyes twinkling in spite of himself at the thought of owning the story of the life of the greatest of heroes, "how much fodder?"

"Wal," said old Josiah, "that book's worth seventy-five cents, at least. You kin earn twenty-five cents a day—that will make three days. You come and pull all you can in three days and you may have the book."

That was an exorbitant price, even if the book were new, but Abe was at the old man's mercy. He realized this, and made the best of a bad bargain. He cheerfully did the work for a man who was mean enough to take advantage of his misfortune. He comforted himself with the thought that he would be the owner of the precious "Life of Washington." Long afterward, in a speech before the New Jersey Legislature, on his way to Washington to be inaugurated, like Washington, as President of the United States, he referred to this strange book.

"THE WHOLE TRUTH AND NOTHING BUT THE TRUTH"

One morning, on his way to work, with an ax on his shoulder, his stepsister, Matilda Johnston, though forbidden by her mother to follow Abe, crept after him, and with a cat-like spring landed between his shoulders and pressed her sharp knees into the small of his back.

Taken unawares, Abe staggered backward and ax and girl fell to the ground together. The sharp implement cut her ankle badly, and mischievous Matilda shrieked with fright and pain when she saw the blood gushing from the wound. Young Lincoln tore a sleeve from his shirt to bandage the gash and bound up the ankle as well as he could. Then he tried to teach the still sobbing girl a lesson.

"'Tilda," he said gently, "I'm surprised. Why did you disobey mother?"

Matilda only wept silently, and the lad went on, "What are you going to tell mother about it?"

"Tell her I did it with the ax," sobbed the young girl. "That will be the truth, too."

"Yes," said Abe severely, "that's the truth, but not *all* the truth. You just tell the whole truth, 'Tilda, and trust mother for the rest."

Matilda went limping home and told her mother the whole story, and the good woman was so sorry for her that, as the girl told Abe that evening, "she didn't even scold me."

"BOUNDING A THOUGHT—NORTH, SOUTH, EAST AND WEST"

Abe sometimes heard things in the simple conversation of friends that disturbed him because they seemed beyond his comprehension. He said of this:

"I remember how, when a child, I used to get irritated when any one talked to me in a way I couldn't understand.

"I do not think I ever got angry with anything else in my life; but that always disturbed my temper—and has ever since.

"I can remember going to my little bedroom, after hearing the neighbors talk of an evening with my father, and spending no small part of the night walking up and down, trying to make out what was the exact meaning of some of their, to me, dark sayings.

"I could not sleep, although I tried to, when I got on such a hunt for an idea; and when I thought I had got it, I was not satisfied until I had repeated it over and over, and had put in language plain enough, as I thought, for any boy I knew to comprehend.

"This was a kind of a passion with me, and it has stuck by me; for I am never easy now when I am bounding a thought, till I have bounded it east, and bounded it west, and bounded it north, and bounded it south."

HIGH PRAISE FROM HIS STEPMOTHER

Not long before her death, Mr. Herndon, Lincoln's law partner, called upon Mrs. Sarah Lincoln to collect material for a "Life of Lincoln" he was preparing to write. This was the best of all the things she related of her illustrious stepson:

"I can say what scarcely one mother in a thousand can say, Abe never gave me a cross word or look, and never refused, in fact or appearance, to do anything I asked him. His mind and mine seemed to run together.

"I had a son, John, who was raised with Abe. Both were good boys, but I must say, both now being dead, that Abe was the best boy I ever saw or expect to see."

"Charity begins at home"—and so do truth and honesty. Abraham Lincoln could not have become so popular all over the world on account of his honest kindheartedness if he had not been loyal, obedient and loving toward those at home. Popularity, also, "begins at home." A mean, disagreeable, dishonest boy may become a king, because he was "to the manner born." But only a good, kind, honest man, considerate of others, can be elected President of the United States.

CHAPTER VII

ABE AND THE NEIGHBORS

"PREACHING" AGAINST CRUELTY TO ANIMALS

Nat Grigsby stated once that writing compositions was not required by Schoolmaster Crawford, but "Abe took it up on his own account," and his first essay was against cruelty to animals.

The boys of the neighborhood made a practice of catching terrapins and laying live coals on their backs. Abe caught a group of them at this cruel sport one day, and rushed to the relief of the helpless turtle. Snatching the shingle that one of the boys was using to handle the coals, he brushed them off the turtle's shell, and with angry tears in his eyes, proceeded to use it on one of the offenders, while he called the rest a lot of cowards.

One day his stepbrother, John Johnston, according to his sister Matilda, "caught a terrapin, brought it to the place where Abe was 'preaching,' threw it against a tree and crushed its shell." Abe then preached against cruelty to animals, contending that "an ant's life is as sweet to it as ours is to us."

ROUGHLY DISCIPLINED FOR BEING "FORWARD"

Abe was compelled to leave school on the slightest pretext to work for the neighbors. He was so big and strong—attaining his full height at seventeen—that his services were more in demand than those of his stepbrother, John Johnston, or of Cousin Dennis. Abe was called lazy because the neighbors shared the idea of Thomas Lincoln, that his reading and studying were only a pretext for shirking. Yet he was never so idle as either Dennis Hanks or John Johnston, who were permitted to go hunting or fishing with Tom Lincoln, while Abe stayed out of school to do the work that one of the three older men should have done.

Abe's father was kinder in many ways to his stepchildren than he was to his own son. This may have been due to the fact that he did not wish to be thought "partial" to his own child. No doubt Abe was "forward." He liked to take part in any discussion, and sometimes he broke into the conversation when his opinion had not been asked. Besides, he got into arguments with his fellow-laborers, and wasted the time belonging to his employer.

One day, according to Dennis, they were all working together in the field, when a man rode up on horseback and asked a question. Abe was the first to mount the fence to answer the stranger and engage him in conversation. To teach his son better "manners" in the presence of his "superiors," Thomas Lincoln struck Abe a heavy blow which knocked him backward off the fence, and silenced him for a time.

Of course, every one present laughed at Abe's discomfiture, and the neighbors approved of Thomas Lincoln's rude act as a matter of discipline. In their opinion Abe Lincoln was getting altogether too smart. While they enjoyed his homely wit and good nature, they did not like to admit that he was in any way their superior. A visitor to Springfield, Ill., will even now find some of Lincoln's old neighbors eager to say "there were a dozen smarter men in this city than Lincoln" when he "happened to get nominated for the presidency!"

SPORTS AND PASTIMES

Abe was "hail fellow, well met" everywhere. The women comprehended his true greatness before the men did so. There was a rough gallantry about him, which, though lacking in "polish," was true, "heart-of-oak" politeness. He wished every one well. His whole life passed with "malice toward none, with charity for all."

When he "went out evenings" Abe Lincoln took the greatest pains to make everybody comfortable and happy. He was sure to bring in the biggest backlog and make the brightest fire. He read "the funniest fortunes" for the young people from the sparks as they flew up the chimney. He was the best helper in paring the apples, shelling the corn and cracking the nuts for the evening's refreshments.

When he went to spelling school, after the first few times, he was not allowed to take part in the spelling match because everybody knew that the side that "chose first" would get Abe Lincoln and he always "spelled down." But he went just the same and had a good time himself if he could add to the enjoyment of the rest.

He went swimming, warm evenings, with the boys, and ran races, jumped and wrestled at noon-times, which was supposed to be given up to eating and resting. He was "the life" of the husking-bee and barn raising, and was always present, often as a judge because of his humor, fairness and tact, at horse races. He engaged heartily in every kind of "manly sport" which did not entail unnecessary suffering upon helpless animals.

Coon hunting, however, was an exception. The coon was a pest and a plague to the farmer, so it should be got rid of. He once told the following story:

THE LITTLE YELLOW "COON DOG"

"My father had a little yellow house dog which invariably gave the alarm if we boys undertook to slip away unobserved after night had set in—as we sometimes did—to go coon hunting. One night my brother, John Johnston, and I, with the usual complement of boys required for a successful coon hunt, took the insignificant little cur with us.

"We located the coveted coon, killed him, and then in a sporting vein, sewed the coon skin on the little dog.

"It struggled vigorously during the operation of sewing on, and when released made a bee-line for home. Some larger dogs on the way, scenting coon, tracked the little animal home and apparently mistaking him for a real coon, speedily demolished him. The next morning, father found, lying in his yard, the lifeless remains of yellow 'Joe,' with strong circumstantial evidence, in the form of fragments of coon skin, against us.

"Father was much incensed at his death, but as John and I, scantily protected from the morning wind, stood shivering in the doorway, we felt assured that little yellow Joe would never again be able to sound the alarm of another coon hunt."

THE "CHIN FLY" AS AN INCENTIVE TO WORK

While he was President, Mr. Lincoln told Henry J. Raymond, the founder of the New York *Times*, the following story of an experience he had about this time, while working with his stepbrother in a cornfield:

"Raymond," said he, "you were brought up on a farm, were you not? Then you know what a 'chin fly' is. My brother and I were plowing corn once, I driving the horse and he holding the plow. The horse was lazy, but on one occasion he rushed across the field so that I, with my long legs, could scarcely keep pace with him. On reaching the end of the furrow I found an enormous chin fly fastened upon the horse and I knocked it off. My brother asked me what I did that for. I told him I didn't want the old horse bitten in that way.

"'Why,' said my brother,'that's all that made him go.'"

"Now if Mr. Chase (the Secretary of the Treasury) has a presidential 'chin fly' biting him, I'm not going to knock it off, if it will only make his department go."

"OLD BLUE NOSE'S" HIRED MAN

It seemed to be the "irony of fate" that Abe should have to work for "Old Blue Nose" as a farm hand. But the lad liked Mrs. Crawford, and Lincoln's sister Nancy lived there, at the same time, as maid-of-all-work. Another attraction, the Crawford family was rich, in Abe's eyes, in possessing several books, which he was glad of the chance to read.

Mrs. Crawford told many things about young Lincoln that might otherwise have been lost. She said "Abe was very polite, in his awkward way, taking off his hat to me and bowing. He was a sensitive lad, never coming where he was not wanted. He was tender and kind—like his sister.

"He liked to hang around and gossip and joke with the women. After he had wasted too much time this way, he would exclaim:

"'Well, this won't buy the child a coat,' and the long-legged hired boy would stride away and catch up with the others."

One day when he was asked to kill a hog, Abe answered promptly that he had never done that, "but if you'll risk the hog, I'll risk myself!"

Mrs. Crawford told also about "going to meeting" in those primitive days:

"At that time we thought it nothing to go eight or ten miles. The ladies did not stop for the want of a shawl or riding dress, or horses. In the winter time they would put on their husbands' old overcoats, wrap up their little ones, and take two or three of them on their beasts, while their husbands would walk.

"In winter time they would hold church in some of the neighbors' houses. At such times they were always treated with the utmost kindness; a basket of apples, or turnips—apples were scarce in those days—was set out. Sometimes potatoes were used for a 'treat.' In old Mr. Linkhorn's (Lincoln's) house a plate of potatoes, washed and pared nicely, was handed around."

FEATS OF STRENGTH

Meanwhile the boy was growing to tall manhood, both in body and in mind. The neighbors, who failed to mark his mental growth, were greatly impressed with his physical strength. The Richardson family, with whom

Abe seemed to have lived as hired man, used to tell marvelous tales of his prowess, some of which may have grown somewhat in the telling. Mr. Richardson declared that the young man could carry as heavy a load as "three ordinary men." He saw Abe pick up and walk away with "a chicken house, made up of poles pinned together, and covered, that weighed at least six hundred if not much more."

When the Richardsons were building their corn-crib, Abe saw three or four men getting ready to carry several huge posts or timbers on "sticks" between them. Watching his chance, he coolly stepped in, shouldered all the timbers at once and walked off alone with them, carrying them to the place desired. He performed these feats off-hand, smiling down in undisguised pleasure as the men around him expressed their amazement. It seemed to appeal to his sense of humor as well as his desire to help others out of their difficulties.

Another neighbor, "old Mr. Wood," said of Abe: "He could strike, with a maul, a heavier blow than any other man. He could sink an ax deeper into wood than any man I ever saw."

Dennis Hanks used to tell that if you heard Abe working in the woods alone, felling trees, you would think three men, at least, were at work there—the trees came crashing down so fast.

On one occasion after he had been threshing wheat for Mr. Turnham, the farmer-constable whose "Revised Statutes of Indiana" Abe had devoured, Lincoln was walking back, late at night from Gentryville, where he and a number of cronies had spent the evening. As the youths were picking their way along the frozen road, they saw a dark object on the ground by the roadside. They found it to be an old sot they knew too well lying there, dead drunk. Lincoln stopped, and the rest, knowing the tenderness of his heart, exclaimed:

"Aw, let him alone, Abe. 'Twon't do him no good. He's made his bed, let him lay in it!"

The rest laughed—for the "bed" was freezing mud. But Abe could see no humor in the situation. The man might be run over, or freeze to death. To abandon any human being in such a plight seemed too monstrous to him. The other young men hurried on in the cold, shrugging their shoulders and shaking their heads—"Poor Abe!—he's a hopeless case," and left Lincoln to do the work of a Good Samaritan alone. He had no beast on which to carry the dead weight of the drunken man, whom he vainly tried, again and again, to arouse to a sense of the predicament he was in. At last the young man took up the apparently lifeless body of the mud-covered man in his strong arms, and carried him a quarter of a mile to a deserted cabin, where he made up a fire and warmed and nursed the old drunkard the rest of that night. Then Abe gave him "a good talking to," and the unfortunate man is said to have been so deeply impressed by the young man's kindness that he heeded the temperance lecture and never again risked his life as he had done that night. When the old man told John Hanks of Abe's Herculean effort to save him, he added:

"It was mighty clever in Abe Lincoln to tote me to a warm fire that cold night."

IN JONES' STORE

While Abe was working for the farmers round about his father's farm he spent many of his evenings in Jones' grocery "talking politics" and other things with the men, who also gathered there. Mr. Jones took a Louisville paper, which young Lincoln read eagerly. Slavery was a live political topic then, and Abe soon acquired quite a reputation as a stump orator.

As he read the "Indiana Statutes" he was supposed to "know more law than the constable." In fact, his taste for the law was so pronounced at that early age that he went, sometimes, fifteen miles to Boonville, as a spectator in the county court. Once he heard a lawyer of ability, named Breckinridge, defend an accused murderer there. It was a great plea; the tall country boy knew it and, pushing through the crowd, reached out his long, coatless arm to congratulate the lawyer, who looked at the awkward youth in amazement and passed on without acknowledging Abe's compliment. The two men met again in Washington, more than thirty years later, under very different circumstances.

But there were things other than politics discussed at the country store, and Abe Lincoln often raised a laugh at the expense of some braggart or bully. There was "Uncle Jimmy" Larkins, who posed as the hero of his own stories. In acknowledgment of Abe's authority as a judge of horse flesh, "Uncle Jimmy" was boasting of his horse's superiority in a recent fox chase. But young Lincoln seemed to pay no heed. Larkins repeated:

"Abe, I've got the best horse in the world; he won the race and never drew a long breath."

Young Lincoln still appeared not to be paying attention. "Uncle Jimmy" persisted. He was bound to make Abe hear. He reiterated:

"I say, Abe, I have got the best horse in the world; after all that running he never drew a long breath."

"Well, Larkins," drawled young Lincoln, "why don't you tell us how many *short* breaths he drew." The laugh was on the boastful and discomfited Larkins.

TRYING TO TEACH ASTRONOMY TO A YOUNG GIRL

Abe's efforts were not always so well received, for he was sometimes misunderstood. The neighbors used to think the Lincoln boy was secretly in love with Kate Roby, the pretty girl he had helped out of a dilemma in the spelling class. Several years after that episode, Abe and Kate were sitting on a log, about sunset, talking:

"Abe," said Kate, "the sun's goin' down."

"Reckon not," Abe answered, "we're coming up, that's all."

"Don't you s'pose I got eyes?"

"Yes, I know you have; but it's the earth that goes round. The sun stands as still as a tree. When we're swung round so we can't see it any more, the light's cut off and we call it night."

"What a fool you are, Abe Lincoln!" exclaimed Kate, who was not to blame for her ignorance, for astronomy had never been taught in Crawford's school.

THE EARLY DEATH OF SISTER NANCY

While brother and sister were working for "Old Blue Nose," Aaron Grigsby, "Nat's" brother, was "paying attention" to Nancy Lincoln. They were soon married. Nancy was only eighteen. When she was nineteen Mrs. Aaron Grigsby died. Her love for Abe had almost amounted to idolatry. In some ways she resembled him. He, in turn, was deeply devoted to his only sister.

The family did not stay long at Pigeon Creek after the loss of Nancy, who was buried, not beside her mother, but with the Grigsbys in the churchyard of the old Pigeon Creek meeting-house.

EARNING HIS FIRST DOLLAR

Much as Abraham Lincoln had "worked out" as a hired man, his father kept the money, as he had a legal right to do, not giving the boy any of the results of his hard labor, for, strong as he was, his pay was only twenty-five or thirty cents a day. Abe accepted this as right and proper. He never complained of it.

After he became President, Lincoln told his Secretary of State the following story of the first dollar he ever had for his own:

"Seward," he said, "did you ever hear how I earned my first dollar?" "No," replied Seward. "Well," said he, "I was about eighteen years of age ... and had constructed a flatboat.... A steamer was going down the river. We have, you know, no wharves on the western streams, and the custom was, if passengers were at any of the landings they had to go out in a boat, the steamer stopping and taking them on board. I was contemplating my new boat, and wondering whether I could make it stronger or improve it in any part, when two men with trunks came down to the shore in carriages, and looking at the different boats, singled out mine, and asked:

"'Who owns this?'

"I answered modestly, 'I do.'

"'Will you,' said one of them, 'take us and our trunks out to the steamer?'

"'Certainly,' said I. I was very glad to have a chance of earning something, and supposed that they would give me a couple of 'bits.' The trunks were put in my boat, the passengers seated themselves on them, and I sculled them out to the steamer. They got on board, and I lifted the trunks and put them on deck. The steamer was moving away when I called out:

"'You have forgotten to pay me.'

"Each of them took from his pocket a silver half-dollar and threw it on the bottom of my boat. I could scarcely believe my eyes as I picked up the money. You may think it was a very little thing, and in these days it seems to me like a trifle, but it was a most important incident in my life. I could scarcely credit that I, a poor boy, had earned a dollar in less than a day—that by honest work I had earned a dollar. I was a more hopeful and thoughtful boy from that time."

CHAPTER VIII

MOVING TO ILLINOIS

"FOLLOWING THE RIVER"

Thomas Lincoln had become restless again. Fourteen years was a long time for him to live in one place. Abe was seven years old when they came over from Kentucky, and he was now nearly twenty-one. During that time Thomas had lost his wife, Nancy, and his only daughter, who bore her mother's name. While the land he had chosen was fertile enough, the want of water had always been a sad drawback. The desire to try his fortunes in a newer country had taken possession of him.

John Hanks had gone to Illinois, and had written back that everything was more favorable there for making a living. Thomas Lincoln had not been successful in Indiana. His children's prospects seemed to be against them. After working as a hired hand on the surrounding farms, Abe had served for a time as a ferryman, and, working by the river, had learned to build the boat with which he had earned his first dollar.

As George Washington longed to go to sea, Abraham Lincoln seems to have yearned to "follow the river." He tried to hire out as deck hand, but his age was against him. He soon had a chance to go "down river" to New Orleans, with his friend, Allen Gentry, the son of the man for whom Gentryville was named. Allen afterward married Kate Roby. A flatboat belonging to Allen's father was loaded with bacon and other farm merchandise for the southern market. Allen went in charge of the expedition, and young Lincoln was engaged as "bow hand." They started in April, 1828. There was nothing to do but steer the unwieldy craft with the current. The flatboat was made to float down stream only. It was to be broken up at New Orleans and sold for lumber.

The two young men from Indiana made the trip without incident until they came to the plantation of Madame Duchesne, six miles from Baton Rouge, where they moored their raft for the night. There they heard the stealthy footsteps of midnight marauders on board.

Young Gentry was first aroused. He sprang up and found a gang of lawless negroes on deck, evidently looking for plunder, and thinking so many of them could easily cow or handle the two white men.

"Bring the guns, Abe!" shouted Allen. "Shoot them!" Abraham Lincoln was among them, brandishing a club—they had no guns. The negroes were frightened not only by the fierce, commanding form of their tall adversary, but also by his giant strength. The two white men routed the whole black crew, but Abraham Lincoln received a wound in the encounter, and bore the scar of it to his dying day.

The trip required about three months, going and returning, and the two adventurers from Gentryville came back in June, with good stories of their experiences to tell in Jones' store.

Not long after this Thomas Lincoln, in response to an urgent invitation from John Hanks, decided to move to Illinois. It took a long time, after gathering in the fall crops, for Thomas Lincoln to have a "vandoo" and sell his corn and hogs. As for selling his farm, it had never really belonged to him. He simply turned it over to Mr. Gentry, who held a mortgage on it. It was February, 1830, before the pioneer wagon got under way. The emigrant family consisted of Thomas Lincoln and Sarah, his wife, Abraham, and John Johnston; Sarah and Matilda Johnston were both married, and, with their husbands, a young man named Hall and Dennis Hanks, formed the rest of the party. The women rode with their household goods in a great covered cart drawn by two yoke of oxen.

A TRAVELING PEDDLER

Merchant Jones, for whom Abe had worked that fall and winter, after his return from New Orleans, sold the young man a pack of "notions" to peddle along the road to Illinois. "A set of knives and forks," related Mr. Jones' son afterward, "was the largest item on the bill. The other items were needles, pins, thread, buttons, and other little domestic necessities. When the Lincolns reached their new home, Abraham wrote back to my father stating that he had doubled his money on his purchases by selling them along the road. Unfortunately we did not keep that letter, not thinking how highly we would prize it afterward."

In the early days of his presidency, an international problem came before the cabinet which reminded Mr. Lincoln of an experience he had on this journey, so he told the several secretaries this story:

"The situation just now reminds me of a fix I got into some thirty years ago when I was peddling 'notions' on the way from Indiana to Illinois. I didn't have a large stock, but I charged large prices and I made money. Perhaps you don't see what I am driving at.

"Just before we left Indiana and were crossing into Illinois we came across a small farmhouse full of children. These ranged in age from seventeen years to seventeen months, and were all in tears. The mother of the family was red-headed and red-faced, and the whip she held in her right hand led to the inference that she had been chastising her brood. The father of the family, a meek-looking, mild-mannered, tow-headed chap, was standing at the front door—to all appearances waiting his turn!

"I thought there wasn't much use in asking the head of that house if she wanted any 'notions.' She was too busy. It was evident that an insurrection had been in progress, but it was pretty well quelled when I got there. She saw me when I came up, and from her look I thought she surmised that I intended to interfere. Advancing to the doorway—roughly pushing her husband aside—she demanded my business.

"'Nothing, ma'am,' I answered as gently as possible. 'I merely dropped in, as I came along, to see how things were going.'

"'Well, you needn't wait,' she said in an irritated way; 'there's trouble here, and lots of it, too, but I kin manage my own affairs without the help of outsiders. This is jest a family row, but I'll teach these brats their places if I hev to lick the hide off every one of them. I don't do much talking, but I run this house, an' I don't want no one sneakin' round tryin' to find out how I do it either.'

"That's the case here with us. We must let the other nations know that we propose to settle our family row in our own way, an' teach these brats (the seceding States) their places, and, like the old woman, we don't want any 'sneakin' round' by other countries, that would like to find out how we are going to do it either."

"WINNING A DOG'S GRATITUDE"

Abe strode along in the mud, driving the four oxen much of the time, for the houses he could visit with his peddler's pack were few and far between. A dog belonging to one of the family—an insignificant little cur—fell behind. After the oxen had floundered through the mud, snow and ice of a prairie stream, they discovered that the animal was missing. The other men of the party thought they could now get rid of the little nuisance, and even the women were anxious, as the hour was late, to go on and find a place to camp for the night. To turn back with the clumsy ox-team and lumbering emigrant wagon was out of the question.

Abraham gave the whip to one of the other men and turned back to see if he could discern the dog anywhere. He discovered it running up and down on the other bank of the river, in great distress, for the swift current was filled with floating ice and the poor little creature was afraid to make the attempt to swim across. After whistling in vain to encourage the dog to try if it would, the tender-hearted youth went to its rescue. Referring to the incident himself afterward, he said:

"I could not endure the idea of abandoning even a dog. Pulling off shoes and socks, I waded across the stream and triumphantly returned with the shivering animal under my arm. His frantic leaps of joy and other evidences of a dog's gratitude amply repaid me for all the exposure I had undergone."

SPLITTING THE HISTORIC RAILS

After two weary weeks of floundering through muddy prairies and jolting over rough forest roads, now and then fording swollen and dangerous streams, the Lincolns were met near Decatur, Illinois, by Cousin John Hanks, and given a hearty welcome. John had chosen a spot not far from his own home, and had the logs all ready to build a cabin for the newcomers. Besides young Abe, with the strength of three, there were five men in the party, so they were able to erect their first home in Illinois without asking the help of the neighbors, as was customary for a "raising" of that kind.

Nicolay and Hay, President Lincoln's private secretaries, in their great life of their chief, gave the following account of the splitting of the rails which afterward became the talk of the civilized world:

"Without the assistance of John Hanks he plowed fifteen acres, and split, from the tall walnut trees of the primeval forest, enough rails to surround them with a fence. Little did either dream, while engaged in this work, that the day would come when the appearance of John Hanks in a public meeting with two of these rails on his shoulder, would electrify a State convention, and kindle throughout the country a contagious and passionate enthusiasm whose results would reach to endless generations."

CHAPTER IX

STARTING OUT FOR HIMSELF

HIS FATHER AND HIS "FREEDOM SUIT"

According to his own account, Abe had made about thirty dollars as a peddler, besides bearing the brunt of the labor of the journey, though there were four grown men in the combined family. As he had passed his twenty-first birthday on the road, he really had the right to claim these profits as his own. His father, who had, for ten years, exacted Abraham's meager, hard-earned wages, should at least have given the boy a part of that thirty dollars for a "freedom suit" of clothes, as was the custom then.

But neither Thomas Lincoln nor his son seems to have thought of such a thing. Instead of entertaining resentment, Abraham stayed by, doing all he could to make his father and stepmother comfortable before he left them altogether. Mrs. Lincoln had two daughters and sons-in-law, besides John Johnston, so Abe might easily have excused himself from looking after the welfare of his parents. Though his father had seemed to favor his stepchildren in preference to his own son, Mrs. Lincoln had been "like an own mother to him," and he never ceased to show his gratitude by being "like an own son to her."

The first work Abe did in that neighborhood was to split a thousand rails for a pair of trousers, at the rate of four hundred rails per yard of "brown jeans dyed with walnut bark." The young man's breeches cost him about four hundred rails more than they would if he had been a man of ordinary height.

But Abraham hovered about, helping clear a little farm, and making the cabin comfortable while he was earning his own "freedom suit." He saw the spring planting done and that a garden was made for his stepmother before he went out of ready reach of the old people.

One special reason Thomas Lincoln had for leaving Indiana was to get away from "the milksick." But the fall of 1830 was a very bad season in Illinois for chills and fever. The father and, in fact, nearly the whole family left at home suffered so much from malaria that they were thoroughly discouraged. The interior of their little cabin was a sorry sight—Thomas and his wife were both afflicted at once, and one married daughter was almost as ill. They were all so sick that Thomas Lincoln registered a shaky but vehement resolve that as soon as they could travel they would "git out o' thar!" He had been so determined to move to Illinois that no persuasion could induce him to give up the project, therefore his disappointment was the more keen and bitter.

The first winter the Lincolns spent in Illinois was memorable for its severity. It is still spoken of in that region as "the winter of the big snow." Cattle and sheep froze to death or died of exposure and starvation.

BUILDING THE FLATBOAT

Early in the spring after "the big snow," John Hanks, Lincoln and John Johnston met Denton Offutt, a man who was to wield an influence on the life of young Lincoln. Offutt engaged the three to take a load of produce and other merchandise to New Orleans to sell. John Hanks, the most reliable member of the Hanks family, gave the following account of the way he managed to bring Abe and his stepbrother into the transaction: "He wanted me to go badly but I waited before answering. I hunted up Abe, and I introduced him and John Johnston, his stepbrother, to Offutt. After some talk we at last made an engagement with Offutt at fifty cents a day and sixty dollars to make the trip to New Orleans. Abe and I came down the Sangamon River in a canoe in March, 1831, and landed at what is now called Jamestown, five miles east of Springfield."

Denton Offutt spent so much time drinking in a tavern at the village of Springfield that the flatboat was not ready when the trio arrived to take it and its cargo down the river. Their employer met them on their arrival with profuse apologies, and the three men were engaged to build the boat and load it up for the journey.

During the four weeks required to build the raft, the men of that neighborhood became acquainted with young Lincoln. A man named John Roll has given this description of Abe's appearance at that time:

"He was a tall, gaunt young man, dressed in a suit of blue homespun, consisting of a roundabout jacket, waistcoat, and breeches which came to within about three inches of his feet. The latter were encased in rawhide boots, into the tops of which, most of the time, his pantaloons were stuffed. He wore a soft felt hat which had once been black, but now, as its owner dryly remarked, 'was sunburned until it was a combine of colors.'"

There was a sawmill in Sangamontown, and it was the custom for the "men folks" of the neighborhood to assemble near it at noon and in the evening, and sit on a peeled log which had been rolled out for the purpose. Young Lincoln soon joined this group and at once became a great favorite because of his stories and jokes. His stories were so funny that "whenever he'd end 'em up in his unexpected way the boys on the log would whoop and roll off." In this way the log was polished smooth as glass, and came to be known in the neighborhood as "Abe's log."

A traveling juggler came one day while the boat was building and gave an exhibition in the house of one of the neighbors. This magician asked for Abe's hat to cook eggs in. Lincoln hesitated, but gave this explanation for his delay: "It was out of respect for the eggs—not care for my hat!"

ABE LINCOLN SAVES THREE LIVES

While they were at work on the flatboat the humorous young stranger from Indiana became the hero of a thrilling adventure, described as follows by John Roll, who was an eye witness to the whole scene:

"It was the spring following 'the winter of the deep snow.' Walter Carman, John Seamon, myself, and at times others of the Carman boys, had helped Abe in building the boat, and when we had finished we went to work to make a dug-out, or canoe, to be used as a small boat with the flat. We found a suitable log about an eighth of a mile up the river, and with our axes went to work under Lincoln's direction. The river was very high, fairly 'booming.' After the dug-out was ready to launch we took it to the edge of the water, and made ready to 'let her go,' when Walter Carman and John Seamon jumped in as the boat struck the water, each one anxious to be the first to get a ride. As they shot out from the shore they found they were unable to make any headway against the strong current. Carman had the paddle, and Seamon was in the stern of the boat. Lincoln shouted to them to head up-stream and 'work back to shore,' but they found themselves powerless against the stream. At last they began to pull for the wreck of an old flatboat, the first ever built on the Sangamon, which had sunk and gone to pieces, leaving one of the stanchions sticking above the water. Just as they reached it Seamon made a grab, and caught hold of the stanchion, when the canoe capsized, leaving Seamon clinging to the old timber and throwing Carman into the stream. It carried him down with the speed of a mill-race. Lincoln raised his voice above the roar of the flood, and yelled to Carman to swim for an elm tree which stood almost in the channel, which the action of the water had changed.

"Carman, being a good swimmer, succeeded in catching a branch, and pulled himself up out of the water, which was very cold, and had almost chilled him to death; and there he sat, shivering and chattering in the tree.

"Lincoln, seeing Carman safe, called out to Seamon to let go the stanchion and swim for the tree. With some hesitation he obeyed, and struck out, while Lincoln cheered and directed him from the bank. As

Seamon neared the tree he made one grab for a branch, and, missing it, went under the water. Another desperate lunge was successful, and he climbed up beside Carman.

"Things were pretty exciting now, for there were two men in the tree, and the boat gone. It was a cold, raw April day, and there was great danger of the men becoming benumbed and falling back into the water. Lincoln called out to them to keep their spirits up and he would save them.

"The village had been alarmed by this time, and many people had come down to the bank. Lincoln procured a rope and tied it to a log. He called all hands to come and help roll the log into the water, and, after this had been done, he, with the assistance of several others, towed it some distance up the stream. A daring young fellow by the name of 'Jim' Dorell then took his seat on the end of the log, and it was pushed out into the current, with the expectation that it would be carried down stream against the tree where Seamon and Carman were.

"The log was well directed, and went straight to the tree; but Jim, in his impatience to help his friends, fell a victim to his good intentions. Making a frantic grab at a branch, he raised himself off the log, which was swept from under him by the raging waters and he soon joined the other victims upon their forlorn perch.

"The excitement on the shore increased, and almost the whole population of the village gathered on the river bank. Lincoln had the log pulled up the stream, and, securing another piece of rope, called to the men in the tree to catch it if they could when he should reach the tree. He then straddled the log himself, and gave the word to push out into the stream. When he dashed into the tree he threw the rope over the stump of a broken limb, and let it play until he broke the speed of the log, and gradually drew it back to the tree, holding it there until the three now nearly frozen men had climbed down and seated themselves astride. He then gave orders to the people on shore to hold fast to the end of the rope which was tied to the log, and leaving his rope in the tree he turned the log adrift. The force of the current, acting against the taut rope, swung the log around against the bank and all 'on board' were saved.

"The excited people who had watched the dangerous expedition with alternate hope and fear, now broke into cheers for Abe Lincoln, and praises for his brave act. This adventure made quite a hero of him along the Sangamon, and the people never tired of telling of the exploit."

"DOWN THE RIVER"

The launching of that flatboat was made a feast-day in the neighborhood. Denton Offutt, its proprietor, was invited to break away from the "Buckhorn" tavern at Springfield to witness the ceremonies, which, of course, took a political turn. There was much speech-making, but Andrew Jackson and the Whig leaders were equally praised.

The boat had been loaded with pork in barrels, corn, and hogs, and it slid into the Sangamon River, then overflowing with the spring "fresh," with a big splash.

The three sturdy navigators, accompanied by Offutt himself, floated away in triumph from the waving crowd on the bank.

The first incident in the voyage occurred the 19th of April, at Rutledge's mill dam at New Salem, where the boat stranded and "hung" there a day and a night.

HOW ABE GOT THE FLATBOAT OVER THE DAM

New Salem was destined to fill an important place in the life of Abraham Lincoln. One who became well acquainted with him described him as the New Salemites first saw him, "wading round on Rutledge's dam with his trousers rolled up nine feet, more or less."

One of the crew gave this account of their mode of operations to get the stranded raft over the dam:

"We unloaded the boat—that is, we transferred the goods from our boat to a borrowed one. We then rolled the barrels forward; Lincoln bored a hole in the end (projecting) over the dam; the water which had leaked in ran out then and we slid over."

Offutt's enthusiasm over Abe's simple method of surmounting this great obstacle was boundless. A crowd had gathered on a hillside to watch Lincoln's operations.

AN IMPROBABLE PROPHECY

For the novelty of the thing, John Hanks claimed to have taken young Lincoln to a "voodoo" negress. She is said to have become excited in reading the future of the tall, thin young man, saying to him, "You will be President, and all the negroes will be free." This story probably originated long afterward, when the strange prophecy had already come true—though fortune tellers often inform young men who come to them that they will be Presidents some day. That such a woman could read the Emancipation Proclamation in that young man's future is not at all likely.

Another story is told of Abraham Lincoln's second visit to New Orleans that is more probable, but even this is not certain to have happened exactly as related. The young northerner doubtless saw negroes in chains, and his spirit, like that of his father and mother, rebelled against this inhumanity. There is little doubt that in such sights, as one of his companions related, "Slavery ran the iron into him then and there."

"I'LL HIT IT HARD!"

But the story goes that the three young fellows—Hanks, Johnston and Lincoln—went wandering about the city, and passed a slave market, where a comely young mulatto girl was offered to the highest bidder. They saw prospective purchasers examine the weeping girl's teeth, pinch her flesh and pull her about as they would a cow or a horse. The whole scene was so revolting that Lincoln recoiled from it with horror and hatred, saying to his two companions, "Boys, let's get away from this. If ever I get a chance to hit that thing"—meaning slavery—"*I'll hit it hard!*"

In June the four men took passage up the river on a steamboat for the return trip. At St. Louis, Offutt got off to purchase stock for a store he proposed to open in New Salem, where he planned to place young Lincoln in charge.

WRESTLING WITH THE COUNTY CHAMPION

The other three started on foot to reach their several homes in Illinois. Abe improved the opportunity to visit his father's family in Coles County, where Thomas Lincoln had removed as soon as he was able to leave their first Illinois home near Decatur.

Abe's reputation as a wrestler had preceded him and the Coles County Champion, Daniel Needham, came and challenged the tall visitor to a friendly contest. Young Lincoln laughingly accepted and threw Needham twice. The crestfallen wrestler's pride was deeply hurt, and he found it hard to give up beaten.

"Lincoln," said he, "you have thrown me twice, but you can't whip me."

Abe laughed again and replied:

"Needham, are you satisfied that I can throw you? If you are not, and must be convinced through a thrashing, I will do that, too—*for your sake!*"

CHAPTER X

CLERKING AND WORKING

HE COULD "MAKE A FEW RABBIT TRACKS"

It was in August, 1831, that Abraham Lincoln appeared in the village of New Salem, Illinois. Neither Denton Offutt nor his merchandise had arrived as promised. While paying the penalty of the punctual man—by waiting for the tardy one—he seemed to the villagers to be loafing. But Abraham Lincoln was no loafer. He always found something useful and helpful to do. This time there was a local election, and one of the clerks had not appeared to perform his duties. A New Salem woman wrote of Lincoln's first act in the village:

"My father, Mentor Graham, was on that day, as usual, appointed to be a clerk, and Mr. McNamee, who was to be the other, was sick and failed to come. They were looking around for a man to fill his place when my father noticed Mr. Lincoln and asked if he could write. He answered that he could 'make a few rabbit tracks.'"

PILOTING A FAMILY FLATBOAT

A few days after the election the young stranger, who had become known by this time as the hero of the flatboat on Rutledge's dam four months before, found employment as a pilot. A citizen, Dr. Nelson, was about to emigrate to Texas. The easiest and best mode of travel in those days was by flatboat down the river. He had loaded all his household goods and movable property on his "private conveyance" and was looking about for a "driver." Young Lincoln, still waiting, unemployed, offered his services and took the Nelson family down the Sangamon River—a more difficult task in August than in April, when the water was high on account of the spring rains. But the young pilot proceeded cautiously down the shallow stream, and reached Beardstown, on the Illinois River, where he was "discharged" and walked back over the hills to New Salem.

ANNOYED BY THE HIGH PRAISES OF HIS EMPLOYER

Denton Offutt and his stock for the store arrived at last, and Lincoln soon had a little store opened for business. A country store seemed too small for a clerk of such astounding abilities, so the too enthusiastic employer bought Cameron's mill with the dam on which Lincoln had already distinguished himself, and made the clerk manager of the whole business.

This was not enough. Offutt sounded the praises of the new clerk to all comers. He claimed that Abraham Lincoln "knew more than any man in the United States." As Mr. Offutt had never shown that he knew enough himself to prove this statement, the neighbors began to resent such rash claims. In addition, Offutt boasted that Abe could "beat the county" running, jumping and wrestling. Here was something the new clerk could prove, if true, so his employer's statement was promptly challenged.

When a strange man came to the village to live, even though no one boasted of his prowess, he was likely to suffer at the hands of the rougher element of the place. It was a sort of rude initiation into their society. These ceremonies were conducted with a savage sense of humor by a gang of rowdies known as the "Clary's Grove Boys," of whom the "best fighter" was Jack Armstrong.

Sometimes "the Boys" nailed up a stranger in a hogshead and it was rolled down hill. Sometimes he was ingeniously insulted, or made to fight in self-defense, and beaten black and blue by the whole gang. They seemed not to be hampered by delicate notions of fair play in their actions toward a stranger. They "picked on him," as chickens, dogs and wolves do upon a newcomer among them.

So when young Lincoln heard his employer bragging about his brain and brawn he was sufficiently acquainted with backwoods nature to know that it boded no good to him. Even then "he knew how to bide his time," and turned it to good account, for he had a good chance, shortly to show the metal that was in him.

"The Boys" called and began to banter with the long-legged clerk in the new store. This led to a challenge and comparison of strength and prowess between young Lincoln and Jack Armstrong. Abe accepted the gauntlet with an alacrity that pleased the crowd, especially the chief of the bully "Boys," who expected an easy victory. But Jack was surprised to find that the stranger was his match—yes, more than his match. Others of "the Boys" saw this, also, and began to interfere by tripping Abe and trying to help their champion by unfair means.

This made young Lincoln angry. Putting forth all his strength, he seized Armstrong by the throat and "nearly choked the exuberant life out of him." When "the Boys" saw the stranger shaking their "best fighter" as if he were a mere child, their enmity gave place to admiration; and when Abe had thrown Jack Armstrong upon the ground, in his wrath, as a lion would throw a dog that had been set upon him, and while the strong stranger stood there, with his back to the wall, challenging the whole gang, with deep-set eyes blazing with indignation, they acknowledged him as their conqueror, and declared that "Abe Lincoln is the cleverest fellow that ever broke into the settlement."

The initiation was over, and young Lincoln's triumph complete. From that day "the Clary's Grove Boys" were his staunch supporters and defenders, and his employer was allowed to go on bragging about his wonderful clerk without hindrance.

GIVING ANOTHER BULLY "A DOSE OF SMARTWEED"

A bumptious stranger came into the store one day and tried to pick a quarrel with the tall clerk. To this end he used language offensive to several women who were there trading. Lincoln quietly asked the fellow to desist as there were "ladies present." The bully considered this an admission that the clerk was afraid of him, so he began to swear and use more offensive language than before. As this was too much for Abraham's patience, he whispered to the fellow that if he would keep quiet till the ladies went out, he (Lincoln) would go and "have it out."

After the women went, the man became violently abusive. Young Lincoln calmly went outside with him, saying: "I see you must be whipped and I suppose I will have to do it." With this he seized the insolent fellow and made short work of him. Throwing the man on the ground, Lincoln sat on him, and, with his long arms, gathered a handful of "smartweed" which grew around them. He then rubbed it into the bully's eyes until he roared with pain. An observer of this incident said afterward:

"Lincoln did all this without a particle of anger, and when the job was finished he went immediately for water, washed his victim's face and did everything he could to alleviate the man's distress. The upshot of the matter was that the fellow became his life-long friend, and was a better man from that day."

HOW HE MADE HIS FELLOW CLERK GIVE UP GAMBLING

Lincoln's morals were unusually good for that time and place. Smoking, chewing, drinking, swearing and gambling were almost universal among his associates. Offutt hired a young man, William G. Greene, after the purchase of the mill. This assistant first told many of the stories, now so well known, concerning Abe at this period of his career:

Young Greene was, like most of the young men in New Salem, addicted to petty gambling. He once related how Lincoln induced him to quit the habit. Abe said to him one day:

"Billy, you ought to stop gambling with Estep." Billy made a lame excuse:

"I'm ninety cents behind, and I can't quit until I win it back."

"I'll help you get that back," urged Lincoln, "if you'll promise me you won't gamble any more."

The youth reflected a moment and made the required promise. Lincoln continued:

"Here are some good hats, and you need a new one. Now, when Estep comes again, you draw him on by degrees, and finally bet him one of these hats that I can lift a forty-gallon barrel of whisky and take a drink out of the bunghole."

Billy agreed, and the two clerks chuckled as they fixed the barrel so that the bunghole would come in the right place to win the bet, though the thing seemed impossible to Greene himself. Estep appeared in due time, and after long parleying and bantering the wager was laid. Lincoln then squatted before the barrel, lifted one end up on one knee, then raised the other end on to the other knee, bent over, and by a Herculean effort, actually succeeded in taking a drink from the bunghole—though he spat it out immediately. "That was the only time," said Greene long afterward, "that I ever saw Abraham Lincoln take a drink of liquor of any kind." This was the more remarkable, as whisky was served on all occasions—even passed around with refreshments at religious meetings, according to Mrs. Josiah Crawford, the woman for whom Abe and Nancy had worked as hired help. Much as Abe disapproved of drinking, he considered that "the end justified the means" employed to break his fellow clerk of the gambling habit.

HOW HE WON THE NAME OF "HONEST ABE"

Abe Lincoln could not endure the thought of cheating any one, even though it had been done unintentionally. One day a woman bought a bill of goods in Offutt's store amounting to something over two dollars. She paid Abe the money and went away satisfied. That night, on going over the sales of the day, Abe found that he had charged the woman six and one-fourth cents too much. After closing the store, though it was late, he could not go home to supper or to bed till he had restored that sixpence to its proper owner. She lived more than two miles away, but that did not matter to Abe

Lincoln. When he had returned the money to the astonished woman he walked back to the village with a long step and a light heart, content with doing his duty.

Another evening, as he was closing the store, a woman came in for a half-pound of tea. He weighed it out for her and took the pay. But early next morning, when he came to "open up," he found the four-ounce weight instead of the eight-ounce on the scales, and inferred that he had given that woman only half as much tea as he had taken the money for. Of course, the woman would never know the difference, and it meant walking several miles and back, but the honest clerk weighed out another quarter pound of tea, locked the store and took that long walk before breakfast. As a "constitutional" it must have been a benefit to his health, for it satisfied his sensitive conscience and soothed his tender heart to "make good" in that way.

Drink and misdirected enthusiasm interfered with Denton Offutt's success. After about a year in New Salem he "busted up," as the neighbors expressed it, and left his creditors in the lurch. Among them was the clerk he had boasted so much about. For a short time Abe Lincoln needed a home, and found a hearty welcome with Jack Armstrong, the best fighter of Clary's Grove!

J. G. Holland wrote, in his "Life of Abraham Lincoln," of the young man's progress during his first year in New Salem:

"The year that Lincoln was in Denton Offutt's store was one of great advance. He had made new and valuable acquaintances, read many books, won multitudes of friends, and become ready for a step further in advance. Those who could appreciate brains respected him, and those whose ideas of a man related to his muscles were devoted to him. It was while he was performing the work of the store that he acquired the nickname, 'Honest Abe'—a characterization that he never dishonored, an abbreviation that he never outgrew. He was everybody's friend, the best-natured, the most sensible, the best-informed, the most modest and unassuming, the kindest, gentlest, roughest, strongest, best fellow in all New Salem and the region round about."

CHAPTER XI

POLITICS, WAR, STOREKEEPING AND STUDYING LAW

STUDYING GRAMMAR FIRST

By "a step still further in advance" Dr. Holland must have meant the young clerk's going into politics. He had made many friends in New Salem, and they reflected back his good-will by urging him to run for the State Legislature. Before doing this he consulted Mentor Graham, the village schoolmaster, with whom he had worked as election clerk when he first came to the place. Abe could read, write and cipher, but he felt that if he should succeed in politics, he would disgrace his office and himself by not speaking and writing English correctly.

The schoolmaster advised: "If you expect to go before the public in any capacity, I think the best thing you can do is to study English grammar."

"If I had a grammar I would commence now," sighed Abe.

Mr. Graham thought one could be found at Vaner's, only six miles away. So Abe got up and started for it as fast as he could stride. In an incredibly short time he returned with a copy of Kirkham's Grammar, and set to work upon it at once. Sometimes he would steal away into the woods, where he could study "out loud" if he desired. He kept up his old habit of sitting up nights to read, and as lights were expensive, the village cooper allowed him to stay in his shop, where he burned the shavings and studied by the blaze as he had done in Indiana, after every one else had gone to bed. So it was not long before young Lincoln, with the aid of Schoolmaster Graham, had mastered the principles of English grammar, and felt himself better equipped to enter politics and public life. Some of his rivals, however, did not trouble themselves about speaking and writing correctly.

GOING INTO POLITICS

James Rutledge, a "substantial" citizen, and the former owner of Rutledge's mill and dam, was the president of the New Salem debating club. Young Lincoln joined this society, and when he first rose to speak, everybody began to smile in anticipation of a funny story, but Abe proceeded to discuss the question before the house in very good form. He was awkward in his movements and gestures at first, and amused those present by thrusting his unwieldy hands deep into his pockets, but his arguments were so well-put and forcible that all who heard him were astonished.

Mr. Rutledge, that night after Abe's maiden effort at the lyceum, told his wife:

"There is more in Abe Lincoln's head than mere wit and fun. He is already a fine speaker. All he needs is culture to fit him for a high position in public life."

But there were occasions enough where something besides culture was required. A man who was present and heard Lincoln's first real stump speech describes his appearance and actions in the following picturesque language:

"He wore a mixed jean coat, clawhammer style, short in the sleeves and bob-tail—in fact, it was so short in the tail that he could not sit upon it— flax and tow linen pantaloons, and a straw hat. I think he wore a vest, but do not remember how it looked. He wore pot metal (top) boots.

"His maiden effort on the stump was a speech on the occasion of a public sale at Pappyville, a village eleven miles from Springfield. After the sale was over and speechmaking had begun, a fight—a 'general fight' as one of the bystanders relates—ensued, and Lincoln, noticing one of his friends about to succumb to the attack of an infuriated ruffian, interposed to prevent it. He did so most effectually. Hastily descending from the rude platform, he edged his way through the crowd, and seizing the bully by the neck and the seat of his trousers, threw him by means of his great strength and long arms, as one witness stoutly insists, 'twelve feet away.' Returning to the stand, and throwing aside his hat, he inaugurated his campaign with the following brief and juicy declaration:

"'Fellow-Citizens: I presume you all know who I am. I am humble Abraham Lincoln. I have been solicited by many friends to become a candidate for the Legislature. My politics are "short and sweet" like the old woman's dance. I am in favor of national bank. I am in favor of the internal improvement system, and a high protective tariff. These are my sentiments and political principles. If elected, I shall be thankful; if not, it will be all the same.'"

The only requirement for a candidate for the Illinois Legislature in 1832 was that he should announce his "sentiments." This Lincoln did, according to custom, in a circular of about two thousand words, rehearsing his experiences on the Sangamon River and in the community of New Salem. For a youth who had just turned twenty-three, who had never been to school a year in his life, who had no political training, and had never made a political speech, it was a bold and dignified document, closing as follows:

"Considering the great degree of modesty which should always attend youth, it is probable I have already been presuming more than becomes me. However, upon the subjects of which I have treated, I have spoken as I have thought. I may be wrong in regard to any or all of them, but, holding it a sound maxim that it is better only sometimes to be right than at all times to be wrong, so soon as I discover my opinions to be erroneous, I shall be ready to renounce them.

"Every man is said to have his peculiar ambition. Whether this is true or not, I can say for one, that I have no other so great as that of being truly esteemed of my fellow-men by rendering myself worthy of their esteem. How far I shall succeed in gratifying this ambition is yet to be developed. I am young and unknown to many of you. I was born, and have ever remained in the most humble walks of life. I have no wealthy or popular relations or friends to recommend me. My case is thrown exclusively upon the independent voters of the country; and, if elected, they will have conferred a favor on me for which I shall be unremitting in my labors to compensate. But if the good people in their wisdom shall see fit to keep me in the background, I have been too familiar with disappointments to be very much chagrined."

"CAPTAIN LINCOLN"

Lincoln had hardly launched in his first political venture when, in April, 1832, a messenger arrived in New Salem with the announcement from Governor Reynolds, of Illinois, that the Sacs and other hostile tribes, led by Black Hawk, had invaded the northern part of the State, spreading terror among the white settlers in that region. The governor called upon those who were willing to help in driving back the Indians to report at Beardstown, on the Illinois River, within a week.

Lincoln and other Sangamon County men went at once to Richmond where a company was formed. The principal candidate for captain was a man named Kirkpatrick, who had treated Lincoln shabbily when Abe, in one of the odd jobs he had done in that region, worked in Kirkpatrick's sawmill. The employer had agreed to buy his hired man a cant-hook for handling the heavy logs. As there was a delay in doing this, Lincoln told him he would handle the logs without the cant-hook if Kirkpatrick would pay him the two dollars that implement would cost. The employer promised to do this, but never gave him the money.

So when Lincoln saw that Kirkpatrick was a candidate for the captaincy, he said to Greene, who had worked with him in Offutt's store:

"Bill, I believe I can make Kirkpatrick pay me that two dollars he owes me on the cant-hook now. I guess I'll run against him for captain."

Therefore Abe Lincoln announced himself as a candidate. The vote was taken in an odd way. It was announced that when the men heard the command to march, each should go and stand by the man he wished to have for captain. The command was given. At the word, "March," three-fourths of the company rallied round Abe Lincoln. More than twenty-five years afterward, when Lincoln was a candidate for the presidency of the United States, he referred to himself in the third person in describing this incident, saying that he was elected "to his own surprise," and "he says he has not since had any success in life which gave him so much satisfaction."

IGNORANCE OF MILITARY TACTICS

But Lincoln was a "raw hand" at military tactics. He used to enjoy telling of his ignorance and the expedients adopted in giving his commands to the company. Once when he was marching, twenty men abreast, across a field it became necessary to pass through a narrow gateway into the next field. He said:

"I could not, for the life of me, remember the word for getting the company *endwise* so that it could go through the gate; so, as we came near the gate, I shouted, 'This company is dismissed for two minutes, when it will fall in again on the other side of the fence.'"

A HISTORIC MYSTERY EXPLAINED

Captain Lincoln had his sword taken from him for shooting within limits. Many have wondered that a man of Lincoln's intelligence should have been guilty of this stupid infraction of ordinary army regulations. Biographers of Lincoln puzzled over this until the secret was explained by William Turley Baker, of Bolivia, Ill., at the Lincoln Centenary in Springfield. All unconscious of solving a historic mystery, "Uncle Billy" Baker related the following story which explains that the shooting was purely accidental:

"My father was roadmaster general in the Black Hawk War. Lincoln used to come often to our house and talk it all over with father, when I was a boy, and I've heard them laugh over their experiences in that war. The best joke of all was this: Father received orders one day to throw log bridges over a certain stream the army had to cross. He felled some tall, slim black walnuts—the only ones he could find there—and the logs were so smooth and round that they were hard to walk on any time. This day it rained and made them very slippery. Half of the soldiers fell into the stream and got a good ducking. Captain Lincoln was one of those that tumbled in. He just laughed and scrambled out as quick as he could. He always made the best of everything like that.

"Well, that evening when the company came to camp, some of them had dog tents—just a big canvas sheet—and the boys laughed to see Lincoln crawl under one of them little tents. He was so long that his head and hands and feet stuck out on all sides. The boys said he looked just like a big terrapin. After he had got himself stowed away for the night, he remembered that he hadn't cleaned his pistol, after he fell into the creek.

"So he backed out from under his canvas shell and started to clean it out. It was what was called a bulldog pistol, because it had a blunt, short muzzle. Abe's forefinger was long enough to use as a ramrod for it. But before he began operations he snapped the trigger and, to his astonishment, the thing went off!

"Pretty soon an orderly came along in great haste, yellin', 'Who did that?—Who fired that shot?' Some of the men tried to send the orderly along about his business, making believe the report was heard further on, but Lincoln he wouldn't stand for no such deception, spoken or unspoken. 'I did it,' says he, beginning to explain how it happened.

"You see, his legs was so blamed long, and he must have landed on his feet, in the creek, and got out of the water without his pistol getting wet, 'way up there in his weskit!

"But he had to pay the penalty just the same, for they took his sword away from him for several days. You see, he was a captain and ought to 'a' set a good example in military discipline."

HOW CAPTAIN LINCOLN SAVED AN INDIAN'S LIFE

One day an old "friendly Indian" came into camp with a "talking paper" or pass from the "big white war chief." The men, with the pioneer idea that "the only good Indian is a dead Indian," were for stringing him up. The poor old red man protested and held the general's letter before their eyes.

"Me good Injun," he kept saying, "white war chief say me good Injun. Look—talking paper—see!"

"Get out! It's a forgery! Shoot him! String him up!" shouted the soldiers angrily.

This noise brought Captain Lincoln out of his tent. At a glance he saw what they were about to do. He jumped in among them, shouting indignantly:

"Stand back, all of you! For shame! I'll fight you all, one after the other, just as you come. Take it out on me if you can, but you shan't hurt this poor old Indian. When a man comes to me for help, he's going to get it, if I have to lick all Sangamon County to give it to him."

The three months for which the men were enlisted soon expired, and Lincoln's captaincy also ended. But he re-enlisted as a private, and remained in the ranks until the end of the war, which found him in Wisconsin, hundreds of miles from New Salem. He and a few companions walked home, as there were not many horses to be had. Lincoln enlivened the long tramp with his fund of stories and jokes.

It is sometimes asserted that Abraham Lincoln and Jefferson Davis met at this early day, as officers in the Black Hawk War, but this statement is not founded on fact, for young Lieutenant Davis was absent on a furlough and could not have encountered the tall captain from the Sangamon then, as many would like to believe.

Lincoln always referred to the Black Hawk War as a humorous adventure. He made a funny speech in Congress describing some of his experiences in this campaign in which he did not take part in a battle, nor did he even catch sight of a hostile Indian.

AGAIN A RIVER PILOT

Abe was still out of work. Just before he enlisted he piloted the *Talisman*, a steamboat which had come up the Sangamon on a trial trip, in which the speed of the boat averaged four miles an hour. At that time the wildest excitement prevailed. The coming of the *Talisman* up their little river was hailed with grand demonstrations and much speech-making. Every one expected the Government to spend millions of dollars to make the Sangamon navigable, and even New Salem (which is not now to be found on the map) was to become a flourishing city, in the hopeful imaginings of its few inhabitants. Lincoln, being a candidate, naturally "took the fever," and shared the delirium that prevailed. He could hardly have done otherwise, even if he had been so disposed. This was before the days of railroads, and the commerce and prosperity of the country depended on making the smaller streams navigable. Lincoln received forty dollars, however, for his services as pilot. The *Talisman*, instead of establishing a river connection with the Mississippi River cities, never came back. She was burned at the wharf in St. Louis, and the navigation of the poor little Sangamon, which was only a shallow creek, was soon forgotten.

LINCOLN'S ONLY DEFEAT BY A DIRECT VOTE

When Abe returned from the war he had no steady employment. On this account, especially, he must have been deeply disappointed to be defeated in the election which took place within two weeks after his arrival. His patriotism had been stronger than his political sagacity. If he had stayed at home to help himself to the Legislature he might have been elected, though he was then a comparative stranger in the county. One of the four representatives chosen was Peter Cartwright, the backwoods preacher.

Lincoln afterward mentioned that this was the only time he was ever defeated by a direct vote of the people.

CHAPTER XII

BUYING AND KEEPING A STORE

After making what he considered a bad beginning politically, young Lincoln was on the lookout for a "business chance." One came to him in a peculiar way. A man named Radford had opened a store in New Salem. Possessing neither the strength nor the sagacity and tact of Abe Lincoln, he was driven out of business by the Clary's Grove Boys, who broke his store fixtures and drank his liquors. In his fright Radford was willing to sell out at almost any price and take most of his pay in promissory notes. He was quickly accommodated. Through William G. Greene a transfer was made at once from Reuben Radford to William Berry and Abraham Lincoln. Berry had $250 in cash and made the first payment. In a few hours after a violent visit from those ruffians from Clary's Grove Berry and Lincoln had formed a partnership and were the nominal owners of a country store.

The new firm soon absorbed the stock and business of another firm, James and Rowan Herndon, who had previously acquired the stock and debts of the predecessors in their business, and all these obligations were passed on with the goods of both the Radford and Herndon stores to "Honest Abe."

The senior partner of the firm of Berry & Lincoln was devoted to the whisky which was found in the inventory of the Radford stock, and the junior partner was given over to the study of a set of "Blackstone's Commentaries," text-books which all lawyers have to study, that came into his possession in a peculiar way, as Candidate Lincoln told an artist who was painting his portrait in 1860:

"One day a man who was migrating to the West drove up in front of my store with a wagon which contained his family and household plunder. He asked me if I would buy an old barrel for which he had no room in his wagon, and which contained nothing of special value. I did not want it, but to oblige him I bought it, and paid him, I think, half a dollar for it. Without further examination I put it away in the store and forgot all about it.

"Some time after, in overhauling things, I came upon the barrel, and emptying it on the floor to see what it contained, I found at the bottom of the rubbish a complete set of 'Blackstone's Commentaries.' I began to read those famous works. I had plenty of time; for during the long summer days, when the farmers were busy with their crops, my customers were few and far between. The more I read the more intensely interested I became.

Never in my whole life was my mind so thoroughly absorbed. I read until I devoured them."

With one partner drinking whisky and the other devouring "Blackstone," it was not surprising that the business "winked out," as Lincoln whimsically expressed it, leaving the conscientious junior partner saddled with the obligations of the former owners of two country stores, and owing an amount so large that Lincoln often referred to it as "the national debt." William Berry, the senior partner, who was equally responsible, "drank himself to death," leaving Lincoln alone to pay all the debts.

According to the custom and conscience of the time, the insolvent young merchant was under no obligation whatever to pay liabilities contracted by the other men, but Lincoln could never be induced even to compromise any of the accounts the others had gone off and left him to settle. "Honest Abe" paid the last cent of his "national debt" nearly twenty years later, after much toil, self-denial and hardship.

POSTMASTER LINCOLN AND JACK ARMSTRONG'S FAMILY

Again out of employment, Abe was forced to accept the hospitality of his friends of whom he now had a large number. While in business with Berry he received the appointment as postmaster. The pay of the New Salem post office was not large, but Lincoln, always longing for news and knowledge, had the privilege of reading the newspapers which passed through his hands. He took so much pains in delivering the letters and papers that came into his charge as postmaster that he anticipated the "special delivery" and "rural free delivery" features of the postal service of the present day.

"A. LINCOLN, DEPUTY SURVEYOR"

Later John Calhoun, the county surveyor, sent word to Lincoln that he would appoint him deputy surveyor of the county if he would accept the position. The young man, greatly astonished, went to Springfield to call on Calhoun and see if the story could be true. Calhoun knew that Lincoln was utterly ignorant of surveying, but told him he might take time to study up. As soon as Lincoln was assured that the appointment did not involve any political obligation—for Calhoun was a Jackson Democrat, and Lincoln was already a staunch Whig—he procured a copy of Flint and Gibson's "Surveying" and went to work with a will. With the aid of Mentor Graham, and studying day and night, he mastered the subject and reported to Calhoun in six weeks. The county surveyor was astounded, but when

Lincoln gave ample proofs of his ability to do field work, the chief surveyor appointed him a deputy and assigned him to the northern part of Sangamon County.

Deputy Surveyor Lincoln had to run deeper in debt for a horse and surveying instruments in order to do this new work. Although he made three dollars a day at it—a large salary for that time—and board and expenses were cheap, he was unable to make money fast enough to satisfy one creditor who was pushing him to pay one of the old debts left by the failure of Berry & Lincoln. This man sued Lincoln and, getting judgment, seized the deputy's horse and instruments. This was like "killing the goose that laid the golden egg." Lincoln was in despair. But a friend, as a surprise, bought in the horse and instruments for one hundred and twenty dollars and presented them to the struggling surveyor.

President Lincoln, many years afterward, generously repaid this man, "Uncle Jimmy" Short, for his friendly act in that hour of need.

Lincoln's reputation as a story teller and wrestler had spread so that when it became known that he was to survey a tract in a certain district the whole neighborhood turned out and held a sort of picnic. Men and boys stood ready to "carry chain," drive stakes, blaze trees, or work for the popular deputy in any capacity—just to hear his funny stories and odd jokes. They had foot races, wrestling matches and other athletic sports, in which the surveyor sometimes took part.

But Lincoln's honesty was as manifest in "running his lines" as in his weights and measures while he was a clerk and storekeeper. In whatever he attempted he did his best. He had that true genius, which is defined as "the ability to take pains." With all his jokes and fun Abraham Lincoln was deeply in earnest. Careless work in making surveys involved the landholders of that part of the country in endless disputes and going to law about boundaries. But Lincoln's surveys were recognized as correct always, so that, although he had mastered the science in six weeks, lawyers and courts had such confidence in his skill, as well as his honesty, that his record as to a certain corner or line was accepted as the true verdict and that ended the dispute.

ELECTED TO THE LEGISLATURE

Hampered though he was by unjust debts and unreasonable creditors, Postmaster and Surveyor Lincoln gained an honorable reputation throughout the county, so that when he ran for the State Legislature, in 1834, he was elected by a creditable majority.

CHAPTER XIII

THE YOUNG LEGISLATOR IN LOVE

SMOOT'S RESPONSIBILITY

Paying his debts had kept Lincoln so poor that, though he had been elected to the Legislature, he was not properly clothed or equipped to make himself presentable as the people's representative at the State capital, then located at Vandalia. One day he went with a friend to call on an older acquaintance, named Smoot, who was almost as dry a joker as himself, but Smoot had more of this world's goods than the young legislator-elect. Lincoln began at once to chaff his friend.

"Smoot," said he, "did you vote for me?"

"I did that very thing," answered Smoot.

"Well," said Lincoln with a wink, "that makes you responsible. You must lend me the money to buy suitable clothing, for I want to make a decent appearance in the Legislature."

"How much do you want?" asked Smoot.

"About two hundred dollars, I reckon."

For friendship's sake and for the honor of Sangamon County the young representative received the money at once.

ANN RUTLEDGE—"LOVED AND LOST"

Abe Lincoln's new suit of clothes made him look still more handsome in the eyes of Ann, the daughter of the proprietor of Rutledge's Tavern, where Abe was boarding at that time. She was a beautiful girl who had been betrothed to a young man named McNamar, who was said to have returned to New York State to care for his dying father and look after the family estate. It began to leak out that this young man was going about under an assumed name and certain suspicious circumstances came to light. But Ann, though she loved the young legislator, still clung to her promise and the man who had proved false to her. As time went on, though she was supposed to be betrothed to Mr. Lincoln, the treatment she had received from the recreant lover preyed upon her mind so that she fell into a decline in the summer of 1835, about a year after her true lover's election to the Legislature.

William O. Stoddard, one of the President's private secretaries, has best told the story of the young lover's despair over the loss of his first love:

"It is not known precisely when Ann Rutledge told her suitor that her heart was his, but early in 1835 it was publicly known that they were solemnly betrothed. Even then the scrupulous maiden waited for the return of the absent McNamar, that she might be formally released from the obligation to him which he had so recklessly forfeited. Her friends argued with her that she was carrying her scruples too far, and at last, as neither man nor letter came, she permitted it to be understood that she would marry Abraham Lincoln as soon as his legal studies should be completed.

"That was a glorious summer for him; the brightest, sweetest, most hopeful he yet had known. It was also the fairest time he was ever to see; for even now, as the golden days came and went, they brought an increasing shadow on their wings. It was a shadow that was not to pass away. Little by little came indications that the health of Ann Rutledge had suffered under the prolonged strain to which she had been subjected. Her sensitive nature had been strung to too high a tension and the chords of her life were beginning to give way.

"There were those of her friends who said that she died of a broken heart, but the doctors called it 'brain fever.'

"On the 25th of August, 1835, just before the summer died, she passed away from earth. But she never faded from the heart of Abraham Lincoln. . . . In her early grave was buried the best hope he ever knew, and the shadow of that great darkness was never entirely lifted from him.

"A few days before Ann's death a message from her brought her betrothed to her bedside, and they were left alone. No one ever knew what passed between them in the endless moments of that last sad farewell; but Lincoln left the house with inexpressible agony written upon his face. He had been to that hour a man of marvelous poise and self-control, but the pain he now struggled with grew deeper and more deep, until, when they came and told him she was dead, his heart and will, and even his brain itself gave way. He was utterly without help or the knowledge of possible help in this world or beyond it. He was frantic for a time, seeming even to lose the sense of his own identity, and all New Salem said that he was insane. He piteously moaned and raved:

"'I never can be reconciled to have the snow, rain, and storms beat upon her grave.'

"His best friends seemed to have lost their influence over him, . . . all but one; for Bowling Green . . . managed to entice the poor fellow to his own home, a short distance from the village, there to keep watch and ward over him until the fury of his sorrow should wear away. There were well-grounded fears lest he might do himself some injury, and the watch was vigilantly kept.

"In a few weeks reason again obtained the mastery, and it was safe to let him return to his studies and his work. He could indeed work again, and he could once more study law, for there was a kind of relief in steady occupation and absorbing toil, but he was not, could not ever be the same man. . . .

"Lincoln had been fond of poetry from boyhood, and had gradually made himself familiar with large parts of Shakespeare's plays and the works of other great writers. He now discovered, in a strange collection of verses, the one poem which seemed best to express the morbid, troubled, sore condition of his mind, . . . the lines by William Knox, beginning:

"'Oh, why should the spirit of mortal be proud?
Like a swift fleeting meteor, a fast flying cloud,
A flash of the lightning, a break of the wave,
He passeth from life to his rest in the grave:'"

"THE LONG NINE" AND THE REMOVAL TO SPRINGFIELD

Two years was the term for which Lincoln was elected to the Legislature. The year following the death of Ann Rutledge he threw himself into a vigorous campaign for re-election. He had found much to do at Vandalia. The greatest thing was the proposed removal of the State capital to Springfield. In this enterprise he had the co-operation of a group of tall men, known as "the Long Nine," of whom he was the tallest and came to be the leader.

Lincoln announced his second candidacy in this brief, informal letter in the county paper:

"NEW SALEM, June 13, 1836.

"TO THE EDITOR OR THE JOURNAL:

"In your paper of last Saturday I see a communication over the signature of 'Many Voters' in which the candidates who are announced in the *Journal* are called upon to 'show their hands.'

"Agreed. Here's mine:

"I go in for all sharing the privileges of the government who assist in bearing its burdens. Consequently, I go for admitting all whites to the right of suffrage who pay taxes or bear arms (by no means excluding females).

"If elected, I shall consider the whole people of Sangamon my constituents, as well those that oppose as those that support me.

"While acting as their Representative, I shall be governed by their will on all subjects upon which I have the means of knowing what their will is; and upon all others I shall do what my own judgment teaches me will best advance their interests. Whether elected or not, I go for distributing the proceeds of public lands to the several States to enable our State, in common with others, to dig canals and construct railroads without borrowing and paying interest on it.

"If alive on the first Monday in November, I shall vote for Hugh L. White for President.

"Very respectfully,
"A. LINCOLN."

The earliest railroads in the United States had been built during the five years just preceding this announcement, the first one of all, only thirteen miles long, near Baltimore, in 1831. It is interesting to observe the enthusiasm with which the young frontier politician caught the progressive idea, and how quickly the minds of the people turned from impossible river "improvements" to the grand possibilities of railway transportation.

Many are the stories of the remarkable Sangamon campaign in 1836. Rowan Herndon, Abe's fellow pilot and storekeeper, told the following:

WINNING VOTES, WIELDING THE "CRADLE" IN A WHEAT FIELD

"Abraham came to my house, near Island Grove, during harvest. There were some thirty men in the field. He got his dinner and went out into the field, where the men were at work. I gave him an introduction, and the boys said that they could not vote for a man unless he could take a hand.

"'Well, boys,' said he, 'if that is all, I am sure of your votes' He took the 'cradle' and led all the way round with perfect ease. The boys were satisfied, and I don't think he lost a vote in the crowd.

"The next day there was speaking at Berlin. He went from my house with Dr. Barnett, who had asked me who this man Lincoln was. I told him that he was a candidate for the Legislature. He laughed and said:

"'Can't the party raise any better material than that?'

"I said, 'Go to-morrow and hear him before you pronounce judgment.'

"When he came back I said, 'Doctor, what do you say now?'

"'Why, sir,' said he, 'he is a perfect "take-in." He knows more than all of them put together.'"

TALKED TO A WOMAN WHILE HIS RIVAL MILKED

Young Lincoln happened to call to speak to a leading farmer in the district, and found his rival, a Democratic candidate, there on the same errand. The farmer was away from home, so each of the candidates did his best to gain the good-will of the farmer's "better half," who was on her way to milk the cow. The Democrat seized the pail and insisted on doing the work for her. Lincoln did not make the slightest objection, but improved the opportunity thus given to chat with their hostess. This he did so successfully that when his rival had finished the unpleasant task, the only acknowledgment he received was a profusion of thanks from the woman for the opportunity he had given her of having "*such a pleasant talk with Mr. Lincoln!*"

HOW THE LIGHTNING STRUCK FORQUER, IN SPITE OF HIS LIGHTNING-ROD

Abe distinguished himself in his first political speech at Springfield, the county seat. A leading citizen there, George Forquer, was accused of changing his political opinions to secure a certain government position; he also had his fine residence protected by the first lightning-rod ever seen in that part of the country.

The contest was close and exciting. There were seven Democratic and seven Whig candidates for the lower branch of the Legislature. Forquer, though not a candidate, asked to be heard in reply to young Lincoln, whom he proceeded to attack in a sneering overbearing way, ridiculing the young man's appearance, dress, manners and so on. Turning to Lincoln who then stood within a few feet of him, Forquer announced his intention in these words: "This young man must be taken down, and I am truly sorry that the task devolves upon me."

The "Clary's Grove Boys," who attended the meeting in a body—or a gang!—could hardly be restrained from arising in their might and smiting the pompous Forquer, hip and thigh.

But their hero, with pale face and flashing eyes, smiled as he shook his head at them, and calmly answered the insulting speech of his opponent. Among other things he said:

"The gentleman commenced his speech by saying 'this young man,' alluding to me, 'must be taken down.' I am not so young in years as I am in the tricks and trades of a politician, but"—pointing at Forquer—"live long or die young, I would rather die now than, like the gentleman, change my politics, and with the change receive an office worth three thousand dollars a year, and then feel obliged to erect a lightning-rod over my house to protect a guilty conscience from an offended God!"

This stroke blasted Forquer's political prospects forever, and satisfied the Clary's Grove Boys that it was even better than all the things they would have done to him.

ABE LINCOLN AS A "BLOATED ARISTOCRAT"

On another occasion Lincoln's wit suddenly turned the tables on an abusive opponent. One of the Democratic orators was Colonel Dick Taylor, a dapper, but bombastic little man, who rode in his carriage, and dressed richly. But, politically, he boasted of belonging to the Democrats, "the bone and sinew, the hard-fisted yeomanry of the land," and sneered at those "rag barons," those Whig aristocrats, the "silk stocking gentry!" As Abe Lincoln, the leading Whig present, was dressed in Kentucky jeans, coarse boots, a checkered shirt without a collar or necktie, and an old slouch hat, Colonel Taylor's attack on the "bloated Whig aristocracy" sounded rather absurd.

Once the colonel made a gesture so violent that it tore his vest open and exposed his elegant shirt ruffles, his gold watch-fob, his seals and other ornaments to the view of all. Before Taylor, in his embarrassment, could adjust his waistcoat, Lincoln stepped to the front exclaiming:

"Behold the hard-fisted Democrat! Look at this specimen of 'bone and sinew'—and here, gentlemen," laying his big work-bronzed hand on his heart and bowing obsequiously—"here, at your service, is your 'aristocrat!' Here is one of your 'silk stocking gentry!'" Then spreading out his great bony hands he continued, "Here is your 'rag baron' with his lily-white hands. Yes, I suppose I am, according to my friend Taylor, a 'bloated aristocrat!'"

The contrast was so ludicrous, and Abe had quoted the speaker's stock phrases with such a marvelous mimicry that the crowd burst into a roar, and Colonel Dick Taylor's usefulness as a campaign speaker was at an end.

Small wonder, then, that young Lincoln's wit, wisdom and power of ridicule made him known in that campaign as one of the greatest orators in the State, or that he was elected by such an astonishing plurality that the county, which had always been strongly Democratic, elected Whig representatives that year.

After Herculean labors "the Long Nine" succeeded in having the State capital removed from Vandalia to Springfield. This move added greatly to the influence and renown of its "prime mover," Abraham Lincoln, who was feasted and "toasted" by the people of Springfield and by politicians all over the State. After reading "Blackstone" during his political campaigns, young Lincoln fell in again with Major John T. Stuart, whom he had met in the Black Hawk War, and who gave him helpful advice and lent him other books that he might "read law."

THE LINCOLN-STONE PROTEST

Although he had no idea of it at the time, Abraham Lincoln took part in a grander movement than the removal of a State capital. Resolutions were adopted in the Legislature in favor of slavery and denouncing the hated "abolitionists"—or people who spoke and wrote for the abolition of slavery. It required true heroism for a young man thus to stand out against the legislators of his State, but Abe Lincoln seems to have thought little of that. The hatred of the people for any one who opposed slavery was very bitter. Lincoln found one man, named Stone, who was willing to sign a protest against the resolutions favoring slavery, which read as follows:

"Resolutions upon the subject of domestic slavery having passed both branches of the General Assembly at its present session, the undersigned hereby protest against the passage of the same.

"They believe that the institution of slavery is founded on both injustice and bad policy. [After several statements of their belief concerning the powers of Congress, the protest closed as follows:]

"The difference between their opinions and those contained in the said resolution is their reason for entering this protest.

"DAN STONE,
"A. LINCOLN."

CHAPTER XIV

MOVING TO SPRINGFIELD

New Salem could no longer give young Lincoln scope for his growing power and influence. Within a few weeks after the Lincoln-Stone protest, late in March, 1837, after living six years in the little village which held so much of life and sorrow for him, Abe sold his surveying compass, marking-pins, chain and pole, packed all his effects into his saddle-bags, borrowed a horse of his good friend "Squire" Bowling Green, and reluctantly said good-bye to his friends there. It is a strange fact that New Salem ceased to exist within a year from the day "Honest Abe" left it. Even its little post office was discontinued by the Government.

Henry C. Whitney, who was associated with Lincoln in those early days, describes Abe's modest entry into the future State capital, with all his possessions in a pair of saddle-bags, and calling at the store of Joshua F. Speed, overlooking "the square," in the following dialogue:

Speed—"Hello, Abe, just from Salem?"

Lincoln—"Howdy, Speed! Yes, this is my first show-up."

Speed—"So you are to be one of us?"

Lincoln—"I reckon so, if you will let me take pot luck with you."

Speed—"All right, Abe; it's better than Salem."

Lincoln—"I've been to Gorman's and got a single bedstead; now you figure out what it will cost for a tick, blankets and so forth."

Speed (after figuring)—"Say, seventeen dollars or so."

Lincoln (countenance paling)—"I had no *idea* it would cost half that, and I—I can't pay it; but if you can wait on me till Christmas, and I make anything, I'll pay; if I don't, I can't."

Speed—"I can do better than that; upstairs I sleep in a bed big enough for two, and you just come and sleep with me till you can do better."

Lincoln (brightening)—"Good, where is it?"

Speed—"Upstairs behind that pile of barrels—turn to the right when you go up."

Lincoln (returning joyously)—"Well, Speed, I've moved!"

STUART & LINCOLN

Major Stuart had grown so thoroughly interested in Lincoln, approving the diligence with which the young law student applied himself to the books which he had lent him, that, after his signal success in bringing about the removal of the State capital to Springfield, the older man invited the younger to go into partnership with him.

Abe had been admitted to the bar the year before, and had practiced law in a small way before Squire Bowling Green in New Salem. Greatly flattered by the offer of such a man, Abe gladly accepted, and soon after his arrival in Springfield this sign, which thrilled the junior partner's whole being, appeared in front of an office near the square:

STUART & LINCOLN
ATTORNEYS-AT-LAW

"I NEVER USE ANYONE'S MONEY BUT MY OWN"

After a while Lincoln left Speed's friendly loft and slept on a lounge in the law office, keeping his few effects in the little old-fashioned trunk pushed out of sight under his couch.

One day an agent of the Post Office Department came in and asked if Abraham Lincoln could be found there. Abe arose and, reaching out his hand, said that was his name. The agent then stated his business; he had come to collect a balance due the Post Office Department since the closing of the post office at New Salem.

The young ex-postmaster looked puzzled for a moment, and a friend, who happened to be present, hastened to his rescue with, "Lincoln, if you are in need of money, let us help you."

Abe made no reply, but, pulling out his little old trunk, he asked the agent how much he owed. The man stated the amount, and he, opening the trunk, took out an old cotton cloth containing coins, which he handed to the official without counting, and it proved to be the exact sum required, over seventeen dollars, evidently the very pieces of money Abe had received while acting as postmaster years before!

After the department agent had receipted for the money and had gone out, Mr. Lincoln quietly remarked:

"I never use anyone's money but my own."

DROPS THROUGH THE CEILING TO DEMAND FREE SPEECH

Stuart & Lincoln's office was, for a time, over a court room, which was used evenings as a hall. There was a square opening in the ceiling of the court room, covered by a trap door in the room overhead where Lincoln slept. One night there was a promiscuous crowd in the hall, and Lincoln's friend, E. D. Baker, was delivering a political harangue. Becoming somewhat excited Baker made an accusation against a well-known newspaper in Springfield, and the remark was resented by several in the audience.

"Pull him down!" yelled one of them as they came up to the platform threatening Baker with personal violence. There was considerable confusion which might become a riot.

Just at this juncture the spectators were astonished to see a pair of long legs dangling from the ceiling and Abraham Lincoln dropped upon the platform. Seizing the water pitcher he took his stand beside the speaker, and brandished it, his face ablaze with indignation.

"Gentlemen," he said, when the confusion had subsided, "let us not disgrace the age and the country in which we live. This is a land where freedom of speech is guaranteed. Mr. Baker has a right to speak, and ought to be permitted to do so. I am here to protect him and no man shall take him from this stand if I can prevent it." Lincoln had opened the trap door in his room and silently watched the proceedings until he saw that his presence was needed below. Then he dropped right into the midst of the fray, and defended his friend and the right of free speech at the same time.

DEFENDING THE DEFENSELESS

A widow came to Mr. Lincoln and told him how an attorney had charged her an exorbitant fee for collecting her pension. Such cases filled him with righteous wrath. He cared nothing for "professional etiquette," if it permitted the swindling of a poor woman. Going directly to the greedy lawyer, he forced him to refund to the widow all that he had charged in excess of a fair fee for his services, or he would start proceedings at once to prevent the extortionate attorney from practicing law any longer at the Springfield bar.

If a negro had been wronged in any way, Lawyer Lincoln was the only attorney in Springfield who dared to appear in his behalf, for he always did so at great risk to his political standing. Sometimes he appeared in defense of fugitive slaves, or negroes who had been freed or had run away from southern or "slave" States where slavery prevailed to gain liberty in "free"

States in which slavery was not allowed. Lawyer Lincoln did all this at the risk of making himself very unpopular with his fellow-attorneys and among the people at large, the greater part of whom were then in favor of permitting those who wished to own, buy and sell negroes as slaves.

Lincoln always sympathized with the poor and down-trodden. He could not bear to charge what his fellow-lawyers considered a fair price for the amount of work and time spent on a case. He often advised those who came to him to settle their disputes without going to law. Once he told a man he would charge him a large fee if he had to try the case, but if the parties in the dispute settled their difficulty without going into court he would furnish them all the legal advice they needed free of charge. Here is some excellent counsel Lawyer Lincoln gave, in later life, in an address to a class of young attorneys:

"Discourage litigation. Persuade your neighbors to compromise whenever you can. Point out to them how the nominal winner is often the real loser—in fees, expenses and waste of time. As a peacemaker a lawyer has a superior opportunity of becoming a good man. There will always be enough business. Never stir up litigation. A worse man can scarcely be found than one who does this. Who can be more nearly a fiend than he who habitually overhauls the register of deeds in search of defects in titles whereon to stir up strife and put money in his pocket. A moral tone ought to be infused into the profession which should drive such men out of it."

YOUNG LAWYER LINCOLN OFFERS TO PAY HALF THE DAMAGES

A wagonmaker in Mechanicsville, near Springfield, was sued on account of a disputed bill. The other side had engaged the best lawyer in the place. The cartwright saw that his own attorney would be unable to defend the case well. So, when the day of the trial arrived he sent his son-in-law to Springfield to bring Mr. Lincoln to save the day for him if possible. He said to the messenger:

"Son, you've just got time. Take this letter to my young friend, Abe Lincoln, and bring him back in the buggy to appear in the case. Guess he'll come if he can."

The young man from Mechanicsville found the lawyer in the street playing "knucks" with a troop of children and laughing heartily at the fun they were all having. When the note was handed to him, Lincoln said:

"All right, wait a minute," and the game soon ended amid peals of laughter. Then the young lawyer jumped into the buggy. On the way back Mr. Lincoln told his companion such funny stories that the young man, convulsed with laughter, was unable to drive. The horse, badly broken, upset them into a ditch, smashing the vehicle.

"You stay behind and look after the buggy," said the lawyer. "I'll walk on."

He came, with long strides, into the court room just in time for the trial and won the case for the wagonmaker.

"What am I to pay you?" asked the client delighted.

"I hope you won't think ten or fifteen dollars too much," said the young attorney, "and I'll pay half the hire of the buggy and half the cost of repairing it."

LAWYER LINCOLN AND MARY OWENS

About the time Mr. Lincoln was admitted to the bar, Miss Mary Owens, a bright and beautiful young woman from Kentucky, came to visit her married sister near New Salem. The sister had boasted that she was going to "make a match" between her sister and Lawyer Lincoln. The newly admitted attorney smiled indulgently at all this banter until he began to consider himself under obligations to marry Miss Owens if that young lady proved willing.

After he went to live in Springfield, with no home but his office, he wrote the young lady a long, discouraging letter, of which this is a part:

"I am thinking of what we said about your coming to live in Springfield. I am afraid you would not be satisfied. There is a great deal of flourishing about in carriages here, which it would be your doom to see without sharing it. You would have to be poor without the means of hiding your poverty. Do you believe that you could bear that patiently? Whatever woman may cast her lot with mine, should any ever do so, it is my intention to do all in my power to make her happy and contented, and there is nothing I can imagine that could make me more unhappy than to fail in that effort. I know I should be much happier with you than the way I am, provided I saw no sign of discontent in you.

"I much wish you would think seriously before you decide. What I have said, I will most positively abide by, provided you wish it. You have not been accustomed to hardship, and it may be more severe than you now imagine. I know you are capable of thinking correctly on any subject, and if you deliberate maturely upon this before you decide, then I am willing to abide by your decision.

"Yours, etc.,
"LINCOLN."

For a love letter this was nearly as cold and formal as a legal document. Miss Owens could see well enough that Lawyer Lincoln was not much in love with her, and she let him know, as kindly as she could, that she was not disposed to cast her lot for life with an enforced lover, as he had proved himself to be. She afterward confided to a friend that "Mr. Lincoln was deficient in those little links which make up the chain of a woman's happiness."

THE EARLY RIVALRY BETWEEN LINCOLN AND DOUGLAS

Soon after Mr. Lincoln came to Springfield he met Stephen A. Douglas, a brilliant little man from Vermont. The two seemed naturally to take opposing sides of every question. They were opposite in every way. Lincoln was tall, angular and awkward. Douglas was small, round and graceful—he came to be known as "the Little Giant." Douglas was a Democrat and favored slavery. Lincoln was a Whig, and strongly opposed that dark institution. Even in petty discussions in Speed's store, the two men seemed to gravitate to opposite sides. A little later they were rivals for the hand of the same young woman.

One night, in a convivial company, Mr. Douglas's attention was directed to the fact that Mr. Lincoln neither smoked nor drank. Considering this a reflection upon his own habits, the little man sneered:

"What, Mr. Lincoln, are you a temperance man?"

"No," replied Lincoln with a smile full of meaning, "I'm not exactly a temperance man, but I am temperate in this, to wit:—I *don't drink!*"

In spite of this remark, Mr. Lincoln *was* an ardent temperance man. One Washington's birthday he delivered a temperance address before the Washingtonian Society of Springfield, on "Charity in Temperance Reform," in which he made a strong comparison between the drink habit and black slavery.

LOGAN & LINCOLN

In 1841 the partnership between Stuart and Lincoln was dissolved and the younger man became a member of the firm of Logan & Lincoln. This was considered a long step in advance for the young lawyer, as Judge Stephen T. Logan was known as one of the leading lawyers in the State. From this senior partner he learned to make the thorough study of his cases that characterized his work throughout his later career.

While in partnership with Logan, Mr. Lincoln was helping a young fellow named "Billy" Herndon, a clerk in his friend Speed's store, advising him in his law studies and promising to give the youth a place in his own office as soon as young Herndon should be fitted to fill it.

WHAT LINCOLN DID WITH HIS FIRST FIVE HUNDRED DOLLAR FEE

During the interim between two partnerships, after he had left Major Stuart, and before he went into the office with Logan, Mr. Lincoln conducted a case alone. He worked very hard and made a brilliant success of it, winning the verdict and a five hundred dollar fee. When an old lawyer friend called on him, Lincoln had the money spread out on the table counting it over.

"Look here, judge," said the young lawyer. "See what a heap of money I've got from that case. Did you ever see anything like it? Why, I never in my life had so much money all at once!"

Then his manner changed, and crossing his long arms on the table he said:

"I have got just five hundred dollars; if it were only seven hundred and fifty I would go and buy a quarter section (160 acres) of land and give it to my old stepmother."

The friend offered to lend him the two hundred and fifty dollars needed. While drawing up the necessary papers, the old judge gave the young lawyer this advice:

"Lincoln, I wouldn't do it quite that way. Your stepmother is getting old, and, in all probability, will not live many years. I would settle the property upon her for use during her lifetime, to revert to you upon her death."

"I shall do no such thing," Lincoln replied with deep feeling. "It is a poor return, at best, for all the good woman's devotion to me, and there is not going to be any half-way business about it."

The dutiful stepson did as he planned. Some years later he was obliged to write to John Johnston, his stepmother's son, appealing to him not to try to induce his mother to sell the land lest the old woman should lose the support he had provided for her in her declining years.

IN LOVE WITH A BELLE FROM LEXINGTON

Lincoln's popularity in Sangamon County, always increasing, was greatly strengthened by the part he had taken in the removal of the capital to Springfield, which was the county seat as well as the State capital. So he was returned to the Legislature, now held in Springfield, time after time, without further effort on his part. He was looked upon as a young man with a great future. While he was in the office with Major Stuart that gentleman's cousin, Miss Mary Todd, a witty, accomplished young lady from Lexington, Kentucky, came to Springfield to visit her sister, wife of Ninian W. Edwards, one of the "Long Nine" in the State Assembly.

Miss Todd was brilliant and gay, a society girl—in every way the opposite of Mr. Lincoln—and he was charmed with everything she said and did. Judge Douglas was one of her numerous admirers, and it is said that the Louisville belle was so flattered by his attentions that she was in doubt, for a time, which suitor to accept. She was an ambitious young woman, having boasted from girlhood that she would one day be mistress of the White House.

To all appearances Douglas was the more likely to fulfill Miss Todd's high ambition. He was a society man, witty in conversation, popular with women as well as with men, and had been to Congress, so he had a national reputation, while Lincoln's was only local, or at most confined to Sangamon County and the Eighth Judicial Circuit of Illinois.

But Mr. Douglas was already addicted to drink, and Miss Todd saw doubtless that he could not go on long at the rapid pace he was keeping up. It is often said that she was in favor of slavery, as some of her relatives who owned slaves, years later, entered the Confederate ranks to fight against the Union. But the remarkable fact that she finally chose Lincoln shows that her sympathies were against slavery, and she thus cut herself off from several members of her own family. With a woman's intuition she saw the true worth of Abraham Lincoln, and before long they were understood to be engaged.

But the young lawyer, after his recent experience with Mary Owens, distrusted his ability to make any woman happy—much less the belle from Louisville, so brilliant, vivacious, well educated and exacting. He seemed to grow morbidly conscious of his shortcomings, and she was high-strung. A misunderstanding arose, and, between such exceptional natures, "the course of true love never did run smooth."

Their engagement, if they were actually betrothed, was broken, and the lawyer-lover was plunged in deep melancholy. He wrote long, morbid letters to his friend Speed, who had returned to Kentucky, and had recently married there. Lincoln even went to Louisville to visit the Speeds, hoping that the change of scene and friendly sympathies and counsel would revive his health and spirits.

In one of his letters Lincoln bemoaned his sad fate and referred to "the fatal 1st of January," probably the date when his engagement or "the understanding" with Mary Todd was broken. From this expression, one of Lincoln's biographers elaborated a damaging fiction, stating that Lincoln and his affianced were to have been married that day, that the wedding supper was ready, that the bride was all dressed for the ceremony, the guests assembled—but the melancholy bridegroom failed to come to his own wedding!

If such a thing had happened in a little town like Springfield in those days, the guests would have told of it, and everybody would have gossiped about it. It would have been a nine days' wonder, and such a great joker as Lincoln would "never have heard the last of it."

THE STRANGE EVENTS LEADING UP TO LINCOLN'S MARRIAGE

After Lincoln's return from visiting the Speeds in Louisville, he threw himself into politics again, not, however, in his own behalf. He declined to be a candidate again for the State Legislature, in which he had served four consecutive terms, covering a period of eight years. He engaged enthusiastically in the "Log Cabin" campaign of 1840, when the country went for "Tippecanoe and Tyler, too," which means that General William Henry Harrison, the hero of the battle of Tippecanoe, and John Tyler were elected President and Vice-President of the United States.

In 1842 the young lawyer had so far recovered from bodily illness and mental unhappiness as to write more cheerful letters to his friend Speed of which two short extracts follow:

"It seems to me that I should have been entirely happy but for the never-absent idea that there is one (Miss Todd) still unhappy whom I have contributed to make so. That still kills my soul. I cannot but reproach myself for even wishing to be happy while she is otherwise. She accompanied a large party on the railroad cars to Jacksonville last Monday, and at her return spoke, so I heard of it, of having 'enjoyed the trip exceedingly.' God be praised for that."

"You will see by the last *Sangamon Journal* that I made a temperance speech on the 22d of February, which I claim that Fanny and you shall read as an act of charity toward me; for I cannot learn that anybody has read it or is likely to. Fortunately it is not long, and I shall deem it a sufficient compliance with my request if one of you listens while the other reads it."

Early the following summer Lincoln wrote for the *Sangamon Journal* a humorous criticism of State Auditor Shields, a vain and "touchy" little man. This was in the form of a story and signed by "Rebecca of the Lost Townships." The article created considerable amusement and might have passed unnoticed by the conceited little auditor if it had not been followed by another, less humorous, but more personal and satirical, signed in the same way, but the second communication was written by two mischievous (if not malicious) girls—Mary Todd and her friend, Julia Jayne. This stinging attack made Shields wild with rage, and he demanded the name of the writer of it. Lincoln told the editor to give Shields *his* name as if he had written both contributions and thus protect the two young ladies. The auditor then challenged the lawyer to fight a duel. Lincoln, averse to dueling, chose absurd weapons, imposed ridiculous conditions and tried to treat the whole affair as a huge joke. When the two came face to face, explanations became possible and the ludicrous duel was avoided. Lincoln's conduct throughout this humiliating affair plainly showed that, while Shields would gladly have killed *him*, he had no intention of injuring the man who had challenged him.

Mary Todd's heart seems to have softened toward the young man who was willing to risk his life for her sake, and the pair, after a long and miserable misunderstanding on both sides, were happily married on the 4th of November, 1842. Their wedding ceremony was the first ever performed in Springfield by the use of the Episcopal ritual.

When one of the guests, bluff old Judge Tom Brown, saw the bridegroom placing the ring on Miss Todd's finger, and repeating after the minister, "With this ring"—"I thee wed"—"and with all"—"my worldly goods"—"I thee endow"—he exclaimed, in a stage whisper:

"Grace to Goshen, Lincoln, the statute fixes all that!"

In a letter to Speed, not long after this event, the happy bridegroom wrote:

"We are not keeping house but boarding at the Globe Tavern, which is very well kept now by a widow lady of the name of Beck. Our rooms are the same Dr. Wallace occupied there, and boarding only costs four dollars a week (for the two). I most heartily wish you and your family will not fail to come. Just let us know the time, a week in advance, and we will have a room prepared for you and we'll all be merry together for a while."

CHAPTER XV

LINCOLN & HERNDON

YOUNG HERNDON'S STRANGE FASCINATION FOR LINCOLN

Lincoln remained in the office with Judge Logan about four years, dissolving partnership in 1845. Meanwhile he was interesting himself in behalf of young William H. Herndon, who, after Speed's removal to Kentucky, had gone to college at Jacksonville, Ill. The young man seemed to be made of the right kind of metal, was industrious, and agreeable, and Mr. Lincoln looked forward to the time when he could have "Billy" with him in a business of his own.

Mrs. Lincoln, with that marvelous instinct which women often possess, opposed her husband's taking Bill Herndon into partnership. While the young man was honest and capable enough, he was neither brilliant nor steady. He contracted the habit of drinking, the bane of Lincoln's business career. As Mr. Lincoln had not yet paid off "the national debt" largely due to his first business partner's drunkenness, it seems rather strange that he did not listen to his wife's admonitions. But young Herndon seems always to have exercised a strange fascination over his older friend and partner.

While yet in partnership with Judge Logan, Mr. Lincoln went into the national campaign of 1844, making speeches in Illinois and Indiana for Henry Clay, to whom he was thoroughly devoted.

Before this campaign Lincoln had written to Mr. Speed:

"We had a meeting of the Whigs of the county here last Monday to appoint delegates to a district convention; and Baker beat me, and got the delegation instructed to go for him. The meeting, in spite of my attempts to decline it, appointed me one of the delegates, so that in getting Baker the nomination I shall be fixed like a fellow who is made a groomsman to a fellow that has cut him out, and is marrying his own dear 'gal.'"

Mr. Lincoln, about this time, was offered the nomination for Governor of Illinois, and declined the honor. Mrs. Lincoln, who had supreme confidence in her husband's ability, tried to make him more self-seeking in his political efforts. He visited his old home in Indiana, making several speeches in that part of the State. It was fourteen years after he and all the family had removed to Illinois. One of his speeches was delivered from the door of a harness shop near Gentryville, and one he made in the "Old

Carter Schoolhouse." After this address he drove home with Mr. Josiah Crawford—"Old Blue Nose" for whom he had "pulled fodder" to pay an exorbitant price for Weems's "Life of Washington," and in whose house his sister and he had lived as hired girl and hired man. He delighted the old friends by asking about everybody, and being interested in the "old swimming-hole," Jones's grocery where he had often argued and "held forth," the saw-pit, the old mill, the blacksmith shop, whose owner, Mr. Baldwin, had told him some of his best stories, and where he once started in to learn the blacksmith's trade. He went around and called on all his former acquaintances who were still living in the neighborhood. His memories were so vivid and his emotions so keen that he wrote a long poem about this, from which the following are three stanzas:

"My childhood's home I see again
And sadden with the view;
And still, as memory crowds the brain,
There's pleasure in it, too.

"Ah, Memory! thou midway world
'Twixt earth and paradise,
Where things decayed and loved ones lost
In dreamy shadows rise.

"And freed from all that's earthy, vile,
Seems hallowed, pure and bright,
Like scenes in some enchanted isle,
All bathed in liquid light."

TRYING TO SAVE BILLY FROM A BAD HABIT

As Mr. Lincoln spent so much of his time away from Springfield he felt that he needed a younger assistant to "keep office" and look after his cases in the different courts. He should not have made "Billy" Herndon an equal partner, but he did so, though the young man had neither the ability nor experience to earn anything like half the income of the office. If Herndon had kept sober and done his best he might have made some return for all that Mr. Lincoln, who treated him like a foster-father, was trying to do for him. But "Billy" did nothing of the sort. He took advantage of his senior partner's absences by going on sprees with several dissipated young men about town.

WHAT LAWYER LINCOLN DID WITH A FAT FEE

A Springfield gentleman relates the following story which shows Lawyer Lincoln's business methods, his unwillingness to charge much for his legal services; and his great longing to save his young partner from the clutches of drink:

"My father," said the neighbor, "was in business, facing the square, not far from the Court House. He had an account with a man who seemed to be doing a good, straight business for years, but the fellow disappeared one night, owing father about $1000. Time went on and father got no trace of the vanished debtor. He considered the account as good as lost.

"But one day, in connection with other business, he told Mr. Lincoln he would give him half of what he could recover of that bad debt. The tall attorney's deep gray eyes twinkled as he said, 'One-half of nought is nothing. I'm neither a shark nor a shyster, Mr. Man. If I should collect it, I would accept only my regular percentage.'

"'But I mean it,' father said earnestly. 'I should consider it as good as finding money in the street.'

"'And "the finder will be liberally rewarded," eh?' said Mr. Lincoln with a laugh.

"'Yes,' my father replied, 'that's about the size of it; and I'm glad if you understand it. The members of the bar here grumble because you charge too little for your professional services, and I'm willing to do my share toward educating you in the right direction.'

"'Well, seein' as it's you,' said Mr. Lincoln with a whimsical smile, 'considering that you're such an intimate friend, I'd do it for *twice* as much as I'd charge a *total stranger!* Is that satisfactory?'

"'I should not be satisfied with giving you less than half the gross amount collected—in this case,' my father insisted. 'I don't see why you are so loath to take what is your due, Mr. Lincoln. You have a family to support and will have to provide for the future of several boys. They need money and are as worthy of it as any other man's wife and sons.'

"Mr. Lincoln put out his big bony hand as if to ward off a blow, exclaiming in a pained tone:

"'That isn't it, Mr. Man. That isn't it. I yield to no man in love to my wife and babies, and I provide enough for them. Most of those who bring their cases to me need the money more than I do. Other lawyers rob them. They act like a pack of wolves. They have no mercy. So when a needy fellow comes to me in his trouble—sometimes it's a poor widow—I can't take much from them. I'm not much of a Shylock. I always try to get them to settle it without going into court. I tell them if they will make it up among themselves I won't charge them anything.'

"'Well, Mr. Lincoln,' said father with a laugh, 'if they were all like you there would be no need of lawyers.'

"'Well,' exclaimed Lawyer Lincoln with a quizzical inflection which meant much. 'Look out for the millennium, Mr. Man—still, as a great favor, I'll charge you a fat fee if I ever find that fellow and can get anything out of him. But that's like promising to give you half of the first dollar I find floating up the Sangamon on a grindstone, isn't it? I'll take a big slice, though, out of the grindstone itself, if you say so,' and the tall attorney went out with the peculiar laugh that afterward became world-famous.

"Not long afterward, while in Bloomington, out on the circuit, Mr. Lincoln ran across the man who had disappeared from Springfield 'between two days,' carrying on an apparently prosperous business under an assumed name. Following the man to his office and managing to talk with him alone, the lawyer, by means of threats, made the man go right to the bank and draw out the whole thousand then. It meant payment in full or the penitentiary. The man understood it and went white as a sheet. In all his sympathy for the poor and needy, Mr. Lincoln had no pity on the flourishing criminal. Money could not purchase the favor of Lincoln.

"Well, I hardly know which half of that thousand dollars father was gladder to get, but I honestly believe he was more pleased on Mr. Lincoln's account than on his own.

"'Let me give you your five hundred dollars before I change my mind,' he said to the attorney.

"'One hundred dollars is all I'll take out of that,' Mr. Lincoln replied emphatically. 'It was no trouble, and—and I haven't earned even that much.'

"'But Mr. Lincoln,' my father demurred, 'you promised to take half.'

"'Yes, but you got my word under false pretenses, as it were. Neither of us had the least idea I would collect the bill even if I ever found the fellow.'

"As he would not accept more than one hundred dollars that day, father wouldn't give him any of the money due, for fear the too scrupulous attorney would give him a receipt in full for collecting. Finally, Mr. Lincoln went away after yielding enough to say he might accept two hundred and fifty dollars sometime in a pinch of some sort.

"The occasion was not long delayed—but it was not because of illness or any special necessity in his own family. His young partner, 'Billy'

Herndon, had been carousing with several of his cronies in a saloon around on Fourth Street, and the gang had broken mirrors, decanters and other things in their drunken spree. The proprietor, tired of such work, had had them all arrested.

"Mr. Lincoln, always alarmed when Billy failed to appear at the usual hour in the morning, went in search of him, and found him and his partners in distress, locked up in the calaboose. The others were helpless, unable to pay or to promise to pay for any of the damages, so it devolved on Mr. Lincoln to raise the whole two hundred and fifty dollars the angry saloon keeper demanded.

"He came into our office out of breath and said sheepishly:

"'I reckon I can use that two-fifty now.'

"'Check or currency?' asked father.

"'Currency, if you've got it handy.'

"'Give Mr. Lincoln two hundred and fifty dollars,' father called to a clerk in the office.

"There was a moment's pause, during which my father refrained from asking any questions, and Mr. Lincoln was in no mood to give information. As soon as the money was brought, the tall attorney seized the bills and stalked out without counting it or saying anything but 'Thankee, Mr. Man,' and hurried diagonally across the square toward the Court House, clutching the precious banknotes in his bony talons.

"Father saw him cross the street so fast that the tails of his long coat stood out straight behind; then go up the Court House steps, two at a time, and disappear.

"We learned afterward what he did with the money. Of course, Bill Herndon was penitent and promised to mend his ways, and, of course, Mr. Lincoln believed him. He took the money very much against his will, even against his principles—thinking it might save his junior partner from the drunkard's grave. But the heart of Abraham Lincoln was hoping against hope."

CHAPTER XVI

HIS KINDNESS OF HEART

PUTTING TWO YOUNG BIRDS BACK IN THE NEST

Mr. Lincoln's tender-heartedness was the subject of much amusement among his fellow attorneys. One day, while out riding with several friends, they missed Lincoln. One of them, having heard the distressed cries of two young birds that had fallen from the nest, surmised that this had something to do with Mr. Lincoln's disappearance. The man was right. Lincoln had hitched his horse and climbed the fence into the thicket where the fledglings were fluttering on the ground in great fright. He caught the young birds and tenderly carried them about until he found their nest. Climbing the tree he put the birdlings back where they belonged. After an hour Mr. Lincoln caught up with his companions, who laughed at him for what they called his "childishness." He answered them earnestly:

"Gentlemen, you may laugh, but I could not have slept tonight if I had not saved those little birds. The mother's cries and theirs would have rung in my ears."

LAWYER LINCOLN, IN A NEW SUIT OF CLOTHES, RESCUING A PIG STUCK IN THE MUD

Lawyer Lincoln rode from one county-seat to another, on the Eighth Judicial Circuit of Illinois, either on the back of a raw-boned horse, or in a rickety buggy drawn by the same old "crowbait," as his legal friends called the animal. The judge and lawyers of the several courts traveled together and whiled away the time chatting and joking. Of course, Abraham Lincoln was in great demand because of his unfailing humor.

One day he appeared in a new suit of clothes. This was such a rare occurrence that the friends made remarks about it. The garments did not fit him very well, and the others felt in duty bound to "say things" which were anything but complimentary.

As they rode along through the mud they were making Lincoln the butt of their gibes. He was not like most jokers, for he could take as well as give, while he could "give as good as he got."

In the course of their "chaffing" they came to a spot about four miles from Paris, Illinois, where they saw a pig stuck in the mud and squealing lustily. The men all laughed at the poor animal and its absurd plight.

"Poor piggy!" exclaimed Mr. Lincoln impulsively. "Let's get him out of that."

The others jeered at the idea. "You'd better do it. You're dressed for the job!" exclaimed one.

"Return to your wallow!" laughed another, pointing in great glee to the wallowing hog and the mudhole.

Lincoln looked at the pig, at the deep mud, then down at his new clothes. Ruefully he rode on with them for some time. But the cries of the helpless animal rang in his ears. He could endure it no longer. Lagging behind the rest, he waited until they had passed a bend in the road. Then he turned and rode back as fast as his poor old horse could carry him through the mud. Dismounting, he surveyed the ground. The pig had struggled until it was almost buried in the mire, and was now too exhausted to move. After studying the case as if it were a problem in civil engineering, he took some rails off the fence beside the road. Building a platform of rails around the now exhausted hog, then taking one rail for a lever and another for a fulcrum, he began gently to pry the fat, helpless creature out of the sticky mud. In doing this he plastered his new suit from head to foot, but he did not care, as long as he could save that pig!

"Now, piggy-wig," he said. "It's you and me for it. You do your part and I'll get you out. Now—'one-two-*three—up-a-daisy!*'"

He smiled grimly as he thought of the jeers and sneers that would be hurled at him if his friends had stayed to watch him at this work.

After long and patient labor he succeeded in loosening the hog and coaxing it to make the attempt to get free. At last, the animal was made to see that it could get out. Making one violent effort it wallowed away and started for the nearest farmhouse, grunting and flopping its ears as it went.

Lawyer Lincoln looked ruefully down at his clothes, then placed all the rails back on the fence as he had found them.

He had to ride the rest of the day alone, for he did not wish to appear before his comrades until the mud on his suit had dried so that it could be brushed off. That night, when they saw him at the tavern, they asked him what he had been doing all day, eying his clothes with suspicious leers and grins. He had to admit that he could not bear to leave that hog to die, and tried to excuse his tender-heartedness to them by adding: "Farmer Jones's children might have had to go barefoot all Winter if he had lost a valuable hog like that!"

"BEING ELECTED TO CONGRESS HAS NOT PLEASED ME AS MUCH AS I EXPECTED"

In 1846 Abraham Lincoln was elected to Congress, defeating the Rev. Peter Cartwright, the famous backwoods preacher, who was elected to the State Legislature fourteen years before, the first time Lincoln was a candidate and the only time he was ever defeated by popular vote. Cartwright had made a vigorous canvass, telling the people that Lincoln was "an aristocrat and an atheist." But, though they had a great respect for Peter Cartwright and his preaching, the people did not believe all that he said against Lincoln, and they elected him. Shortly after this he wrote again to Speed:

"You, no doubt, assign the suspension of our correspondence to the true philosophic cause; though it must be confessed by both of us that this is a rather cold reason for allowing such a friendship as ours to die out by degrees.

"Being elected to Congress, though I am very grateful to our friends for having done it, has not pleased me as much as I expected."

In the same letter he imparted to his friend some information which seems to have been much more interesting to him than being elected to Congress:

"We have another boy, born the 10th of March (1846). He is very much such a child as Bob was at his age, rather of a longer order. Bob is 'short and low,' and I expect always will be. He talks very plainly, almost as plainly as anybody. He is quite smart enough. I sometimes fear he is one of the little rare-ripe sort that are smarter at five than ever after.

"Since I began this letter, a messenger came to tell me Bob was lost; but by the time I reached the house his mother had found him and had him whipped, and by now very likely he has run away again!

"As ever yours,
"A. LINCOLN."

The new baby mentioned in this letter was Edward, who died in 1850, before his fourth birthday. "Bob," or Robert, the eldest of the Lincoln's four children, was born in 1843. William, born in 1850, died in the White House. The youngest was born in 1853, after the death of Thomas Lincoln, so he was named for his grandfather, but he was known only by his nickname, "Tad." "Little Tad" was his father's constant companion during the terrible years of the Civil War, especially after Willie's death, in 1862. "Tad" became "the child of the nation." He died in Chicago, July 10, 1871, at the age of eighteen, after returning from Europe with his widowed mother and his brother Robert. Robert has served his country as Secretary of War and Ambassador to the English court, and is recognized as a leader in national affairs.

When Lincoln was sent to the national House of Representatives, Douglas was elected to the Senate for the first time. Lincoln was the only Whig from Illinois. This shows his great personal popularity. Daniel Webster was then living in the national capital, and Congressman Lincoln stopped once at Ashland, Ky., on his way to Washington to visit the idol of the Whigs, Henry Clay.

As soon as Lincoln was elected, an editor wrote to ask him for a biographical sketch of himself for the "Congressional Directory." This is all Mr. Lincoln wrote—in a blank form sent for the purpose:

"Born February 12, 1809, in Hardin County, Kentucky.

"Education defective.

"Profession, lawyer.

"Military service, captain of volunteers in Black Hawk War.

"Offices held: Postmaster at a very small office; four times a member of the Illinois Legislature, and elected to the lower House of the next Congress."

Mr. Lincoln was in Congress while the Mexican War was in progress, and there was much discussion over President Polk's action in declaring that war.

As Mrs. Lincoln was obliged to stay in Springfield to care for her two little boys, Congressman Lincoln lived in a Washington boarding-house. He soon gained the reputation of telling the best stories at the capital. He made a humorous speech on General Cass, comparing the general's army experiences with his own in the Black Hawk War. He also drafted a bill to abolish slavery in the District of Columbia, which was never brought to a vote. Most of his care seems to have been for Billy Herndon, who wrote complaining letters to him about the "old men" in Springfield who were always trying to "keep the young men down." Here are two of Mr. Lincoln's replies:

"WASHINGTON, June 22, 1848.

"DEAR WILLIAM:

"Judge how heart-rending it was to come to my room and find and read your discouraging letter of the 15th. Now, as to the young men, you must not wait to be brought forward by the older men. For instance, do you suppose that I would ever have got into notice if I had waited to be hunted up and pushed forward by older men?"

"Dear William:

"Your letter was received last night. The subject of that letter is exceedingly painful to me; and I cannot but think that there is some mistake in your impression of the motives of the old men. Of course I cannot demonstrate what I say; but I was young once, and I am sure I was never ungenerously thrust back. I hardly know what to say. The way for a young man to rise is to improve himself every way he can, never suspecting that anybody wishes to hinder him. Allow me to assure you that suspicion and jealousy never did keep any man in any situation. There may be sometimes ungenerous attempts to keep a young man down; and they will succeed, too, if he allows his mind to be diverted from its true channel to brood over the attempted injury. Cast about, and see if this feeling has not injured every person you have ever known to fall into it.

"Now in what I have said, I am sure you will suspect nothing but sincere friendship. I would save you from a fatal error. You have been a laborious, studious young man. You are far better informed on almost all subjects than I have ever been. You cannot fail in any laudable object, unless you allow your mind to be improperly directed. I have somewhat the advantage of you in the world's experience, merely by being older; and it is this that induces me to advise.

"Your friend, as ever,
"A. Lincoln."

LAST DAYS OF THOMAS LINCOLN

Mr. Lincoln did not allow his name to be used as a candidate for re-election, as there were other men in the congressional district who deserved the honor of going to Washington as much as he. On his way home from Washington, after the last session of the Thirtieth Congress, he visited New England, where he made a few speeches, and stopped at Niagara Falls, which impressed him so strongly that he wrote a lecture on the subject.

After returning home he made a flying visit to Washington to enter his patent steamboat, equipped so that it would navigate shallow western rivers. This boat, he told a friend, "would go where the ground is a little damp." The model of Lincoln's steamboat is one of the sights of the Patent Office to this day.

After Mr. Lincoln had settled down to his law business, permanently, as he hoped, his former fellow-clerk, William G. Greene, having business in Coles County, went to "Goosenest Prairie" to call on Abe's father and stepmother, who still lived in a log cabin. Thomas Lincoln received his son's friend very hospitably. During the young man's visit, the father reverted to the old subject, his disapproval of his son's wasting his time in study. He said:

"I s'pose Abe's still a-foolin' hisself with eddication. I tried to stop it, but he's got that fool *idee* in his head an' it can't be got out. Now I haint got no eddication, but I git along better than if I had."

Not long after this, in 1851, Abraham learned that his father was very ill. As he could not leave Springfield then, he wrote to his stepbrother (for Thomas Lincoln could not read) the following comforting letter to be read to his father:

"I sincerely hope father may recover his health; but at all events, tell him to remember to call upon and confide in our great and merciful Maker, who will not turn away from him in any extremity. He notes the fall of the sparrow, and numbers the hairs of our heads, and He will not forget the dying man who puts his trust in Him. Say to him that, if we could meet now, it is doubtful whether it would be more painful than pleasant, but if it is his lot to go now, he will soon have a joyful meeting with the loved ones gone before, and where the rest of us, through the mercy of God, hope ere long to join them."

Thomas Lincoln died that year, at the age of seventy-three.

A KIND BUT MASTERFUL LETTER TO HIS STEPBROTHER

After his father's death Abraham Lincoln had, on several occasions, to protect his stepmother against the schemes of her own lazy, good-for-nothing son. Here is one of the letters written, at this time, to his stepbrother, John Johnston:

"DEAR BROTHER: I hear that you were anxious to sell the land where you live, and move to Missouri. What can you do in Missouri better than here? Is the land any richer? Can you there, any more than here, raise corn and wheat and oats without work? Will anybody there, any more than here, do your work for you? If you intend to go to work, there is no better place than right where you are; if you do not intend to go to work, you cannot get along anywhere. Squirming and crawling about from place to place can do no good. You have raised no crop this year, and what you really want is to sell the land, get the money and spend it. Part with the land you have and, my life upon it, you will never own a spot big enough to bury you in. Half you will get for the land you will spend in moving to Missouri, and the other half you will eat and drink and wear out, and no foot of land will be bought.

"Now, I feel that it is my duty to have no hand in such a piece of foolery. I feel it is so even on your own account, and particularly on mother's account.

"Now do not misunderstand this letter. I do not write it in any unkindness. I write it in order, if possible, to get you to face the truth, which truth is, you are destitute because you have idled away your time. Your thousand pretenses deceive nobody but yourself. Go to work is the only cure for your case."

CHAPTER XVII

WHAT MADE THE DIFFERENCE BETWEEN ABRAHAM LINCOLN AND HIS STEPBROTHER

These letters show the wide difference between the real lives of two boys brought up in the same surroundings, and under similar conditions. The advantages were in John Johnston's favor. He and Dennis Hanks never rose above the lower level of poverty and ignorance. John was looked down upon by the poor illiterates around him as a lazy, good-for-nothing fellow, and Dennis Hanks was known to be careless about telling the truth.

In speaking of the early life of Abe's father and mother, Dennis threw in the remark that "the Hankses was some smarter than the Lincolns." It was not "smartness" that made Abe Lincoln grow to be a greater man than Dennis Hanks. There are men in Springfield to-day who say, "There were a dozen smarter men in this town than Mr. Lincoln when he happened to be nominated, and peculiar conditions prevailing at that time brought about his election to the presidency!"

True greatness is made of goodness rather than smartness. Abraham Lincoln was honest with himself while a boy and a man, and it was "Honest Abe" who became President of the United States. The people loved him for his big heart—because he loved them more than he loved himself and they knew it. In his second inaugural address as President he used this expression: "With malice toward none, with charity for all." This was not a new thought, but it was full of meaning to the country because little Abe Lincoln had *lived* that idea all his life, with his own family, his friends, acquaintances, and employers. He became the most beloved man in the world, in his own or any other time, because he himself loved everybody.

Mrs. Crawford, the wife of "Old Blue Nose," used to laugh at the very idea of Abe Lincoln ever becoming President. Lincoln often said to her: "I'll get ready and the time will come." He got ready in his father's log hut and when the door of opportunity opened he walked right into the White House. He "made himself at home" there, because he had only to go on in the same way after he became the "servant of the people" that he had followed when he was "Old Blue Nose's" hired boy and man.

ONE PARTNER IN THE WHITE HOUSE, THE OTHER IN THE POOR HOUSE

Then there was William H. Herndon, known to the world only because he happened to be "Lincoln's law partner." His advantages were superior to Lincoln's. And far more than that, he had his great partner's help to push him forward and upward. But "poor Billy" had an unfortunate appetite. He could not deny himself, though it always made him ashamed and miserable. It dragged him down, down from "the President's partner" to the gutter. That was not all. When he asked his old partner to give him a government appointment which he had, for years, been making himself wholly unworthy to fill, President Lincoln, much as he had loved Billy all along, could not give it to him. It grieved Mr. Lincoln's great heart to refuse Billy anything. But Herndon did not blame himself for all that. He spent the rest of his wretched life in bitterness and spite—avenging himself on his noble benefactor by putting untruths into the "Life of Lincoln" he was able to write because Abraham Lincoln, against the advice of his wife and friends, had insisted on keeping him close to his heart. It is a terrible thing—that spirit of spite! Among many good and true things he *had* to say about his fatherly law partner, he poisoned the good name of Abraham Lincoln in the minds of millions, by writing stealthy slander about Lincoln's mother and wife, and made many people believe that the most religious of men at heart was an infidel (because he himself was one!), that Mr. Lincoln sometimes acted from unworthy and unpatriotic motives, and that he failed to come to his own wedding. If these things had been true it would have been wrong to publish them to the prejudice of a great man's good name— then how much more wicked to invent and spread broadcast falsehoods which hurt the heart and injure the mind of the whole world—just to spite the memory of the best friend a man ever had!

The fate of the firm of Lincoln & Herndon shows in a striking way how the world looks upon the heart that hates and the heart that loves, for the hateful junior partner died miserably in an almshouse, but the senior was crowned with immortal martyrdom in the White House.

THE RIVAL FOR LOVE AND HONORS

Stephen A. Douglas, "the Little Giant," who had been a rival for the hand of the fascinating Mary Todd, was also Lincoln's chief opponent in politics. Douglas was small and brilliant; used to society ways, he seemed always to keep ahead of his tall, uncouth, plodding competitor. After going to Congress, Mr. Lincoln was encouraged to aspire even higher, so, ten years later, he became a candidate for the Senate. Slavery was then the burning question, and Douglas seemed naturally to fall upon the opposite side, favoring and justifying it in every way he could.

Douglas was then a member of the Senate, but the opposing party nominated Lincoln to succeed him, while "the Little Giant" had been renominated to succeed himself. Douglas sneered at his tall opponent, trying to "damn him with faint praise" by referring to him as "a kind, amiable and intelligent gentleman." Mr. Lincoln challenged the Senator to discuss the issues of the hour in a series of debates.

Douglas was forced, very much against his will, to accept, and the debates took place in seven towns scattered over the State of Illinois, from August 21st to October 15th, 1858. Lincoln had announced his belief that "a house divided against itself cannot stand;" therefore the United States could not long exist "half slave and half free."

"The Little Giant" drove from place to place in great style, traveling with an escort of influential friends. These discussions, known in history as the "Lincoln-Douglas Debates," rose to national importance while they were in progress, by attracting the attention, in the newspapers, of voters all over the country. They were attended, on an average, by ten thousand persons each, both men being accompanied by bands and people carrying banners and what Mr. Lincoln called "fizzlegigs and fireworks."

Some of the banners were humorous.

```
Abe the Giant-Killer
```

was one. Another read:

```
Westward the Star of Empire takes its way;
The girls link on to Lincoln, their mothers were for Clay.
```

At the first debate Lincoln took off his linen duster and, handing it to a bystander, said:

"Hold my coat while I stone Stephen!"

In the course of these debates Lincoln propounded questions for Mr. Douglas to answer. Brilliant as "the Little Giant" was, he was not shrewd enough to defend himself from the shafts of his opponent's wit and logic. So he fell into Lincoln's trap.

"If he does that," said Lincoln, "he may be Senator, but he can never be President. I am after larger game. The battle of 1860 is worth a hundred of this."

This prophecy proved true.

CHAPTER XVIII

HOW EMANCIPATION CAME TO PASS

When Abraham Lincoln was a small boy he began to show the keenest sympathy for the helpless and oppressed. The only time he betrayed anger as a child was, as you already have learned, when he saw the other boys hurting a mud-turtle. In his first school "composition," on "Cruelty to Animals," his stepsister remembers this sentence: "An ant's life is as sweet to it as ours is to us."

As you have read on an earlier page, when Abe grew to be a big, strong boy he saved a drunken man from freezing in the mud, by carrying him to a cabin, building a fire, and spent the rest of the night warming and sobering him up. Instead of leaving the drunkard to the fate the other fellows thought he deserved, Abe Lincoln, through pity for the helpless, rescued a fellow-being not only from mud and cold but also from a drunkard's grave. For that tall lad's love and mercy revealed to the poor creature the terrible slavery of which he was the victim. Thus Abe helped him throw off the shackles of drink and made a man of him.

BLACK SLAVES AND WHITE

As he grew older, Abe Lincoln saw that the drink habit was a sort of human slavery. He delivered an address before the Washingtonian (Temperance) Society in which he compared white slavery with black, in which he said:

"And when the victory shall be complete—when there shall be neither a slave nor a drunkard on the earth—how proud the title of that land which may truly claim to be the birthplace and the cradle of both those revolutions that have ended in that victory."

This address was delivered on Washington's Birthday, 1842. The closing words throb with young Lawyer Lincoln's fervent patriotism:

"This is the one hundred and tenth anniversary of the birth of Washington; we are met to celebrate this day. Washington is the mightiest name of earth, long since the mightiest in the cause of civil liberty, still mightiest in moral reformation. On that name no eulogy is expected. It cannot be. To add to the brightness of the sun or glory to the name of Washington is alike impossible. Let none attempt it. In solemn awe we pronounce the name and, in its naked, deathless splendor, leave it shining on."

It was young Lincoln's patriotic love for George Washington which did so much to bring about, in time, a double emancipation from white slavery and black.

Once, as President, he said to a boy who had just signed the temperance pledge:

"Now, Sonny, keep that pledge and it will be the best act of your life."

President Lincoln was true and consistent in his temperance principles. In March, 1864, he went by steamboat with his wife and "Little Tad," to visit General Grant at his headquarters at City Point, Virginia.

When asked how he was, during the reception which followed his arrival there, the President said, as related by General Horace Porter:

"'I am not feeling very well. I got pretty badly shaken up on the bay coming down, and am not altogether over it yet.'

"'Let me send for a bottle of champagne for you, Mr. President,' said a staff-officer, 'that's the best remedy I know of for sea-sickness.'

"'No, no, my young friend,' replied the President, 'I've seen many a man in my time seasick ashore from drinking that very article.'

"That was the last time any one screwed up sufficient courage to offer him wine."

"THE UNDER DOG"

Some people are kinder to dumb animals—is it *because* they are dumb?—than to their relatives. Many are the stories of Lincoln's tenderness to beasts and birds. But his kindness did not stop there, nor with his brothers and sisters in white. He recognized his close relationship with the black man, and the bitterest name his enemies called him—worse in their minds than "fool," "clown," "imbecile" or "gorilla"—was a "Black Republican." That terrible phobia against the negro only enlisted Abraham Lincoln's sympathies the more. He appeared in court in behalf of colored people, time and again. The more bitter the hatred and oppression of others, the more they needed his sympathetic help, the more certain they were to receive it.

"My sympathies are with the under dog," said Mr. Lincoln, one day, "though it is often that dog that starts the fuss."

The fact that the poor fellow may have brought the trouble upon himself did not make him forfeit Abraham Lincoln's sympathy. That was only a good lesson to him to "Look out and do better next time!"

THE QUESTION OF EMANCIPATION

After he went to Washington, President Lincoln was between two fires. One side wanted the slaves freed whether the Union was broken up or not. They could not see that declaring them free would have but little effect, if the government could not "back up" such a declaration.

The other party did not wish the matter tampered with, as cheap labor was necessary for raising cotton, sugar and other products on which the living of millions of people depended.

The extreme Abolitionists, who wished slavery abolished, whether or no, sent men to tell the President that if he did not free the slaves he was a coward and a turncoat, and they would withhold their support from the Government and the Army.

Delegations of Abolitionists from all over the North arrived almost daily from different cities to urge, coax and threaten the President. They did not know that he was trying to keep the Border States of Maryland, Kentucky and Missouri from seceding. If Maryland alone had gone out of the Union, Washington, the national capital, would have been surrounded and forced to surrender.

Besides, at this time, the armies of the North were losing nearly all the battles.

To declare all the slaves down South freed, when the Government could not enforce such a statement and could not even win a battle, would be absurd. To one committee the President said: "If I issued a proclamation of emancipation now it would be like the Pope's bull (or decree) against the comet!"

A delegation of Chicago ministers came to beg Mr. Lincoln to free the slaves. He patiently explained to them that his declaring them free would not make them free. These men seemed to see the point and were retiring, disappointed, when one of them returned to him and whispered solemnly:

"What you have said to us, Mr. President, compels me to say to you in reply that it is a message from our divine Master, through me, commanding you, sir, to open the doors of bondage that the slave may go free!"

"Now, isn't that strange?" the President replied instantly. "Here I am, studying this question, day and night, and God has placed it upon me, too.

Don't you think it's rather odd that He should send such a message by way of that awful wicked city of Chicago?"

The ministers were shocked at such an answer from the President of the United States. They could not know, for Mr. Lincoln dared not tell them, that he had the Emancipation Proclamation in his pocket waiting for a Federal victory before he could issue it!

THE PROCLAMATION

Then, came the news of Antietam, a terrible battle, but gained by the Northern arms. At last the time had come to announce the freeing of the slaves that they might help in winning their liberties. The President had not held a meeting of his Cabinet for some time. He thought of the occasion when, as a young man he went on a flatboat trip to New Orleans and saw, for the first, the horrors of negro slavery, and said to his companions:

"If ever I get a chance to hit that thing I'll hit it hard!"

Now the "chance to hit that thing"—the inhuman monster of human slavery—had come, and he was going to "hit it hard."

He called the Cabinet together. Edwin M. Stanton, the Secretary of War, has described the scene:

"On the 22nd of September, 1862, I had a sudden and peremptory call to a Cabinet meeting at the White House. I went immediately and found the historic War Cabinet of Abraham Lincoln assembled, every member being present. The President hardly noticed me as I came in. He was reading a book of some kind which seemed to amuse him. It was a little book. He finally turned to us and said:

"'Gentlemen, did you ever read anything from "Artemus Ward?" Let me read you a chapter that is very funny.'

"Not a member of the Cabinet smiled; as for myself, I was angry, and looked to see what the President meant. It seemed to me like buffoonery. He, however, concluded to read us a chapter from 'Artemus Ward,' which he did with great deliberation. Having finished, he laughed heartily, without a member of the Cabinet joining in the laughter.

"'Well,' he said, 'let's have another chapter.'

"I was considering whether I should rise and leave the meeting abruptly, when he threw the book down, heaved a long sigh, and said:

"'Gentlemen, why don't you laugh? With the fearful strain that is upon me night and day, if I did not laugh I should die, and you need this medicine as much as I do.'

"He then put his hand in his tall hat that sat upon the table, and pulled out a little paper. Turning to the members of the Cabinet, he said:

"'Gentlemen, I have called you here upon very important business. I have prepared a little paper of much significance. I have made up my mind that this paper is to issue; that the time is come when it should issue; that the people are ready for it to issue.

"'It is due to my Cabinet that you should be the first to hear and know of it, and if any of you have any suggestions to make as to the form of this paper or its composition, I shall be glad to hear them. But the paper is to issue.'

"And, to my astonishment, he read the Emancipation Proclamation of that date, which was to take effect the first of January following."

Secretary Stanton continued: "I have always tried to be calm, but I think I lost my calmness for a moment, and with great enthusiasm I arose, approached the President, extended my hand and said:

"'Mr. President, if the reading of chapters of "Artemus Ward" is a prelude to such a deed as this, the book should be filed among the archives of the nation, and the author should be canonized. Henceforth I see the light and the country is saved.'

"And all said 'Amen!'

"And Lincoln said to me in a droll way, just as I was leaving, 'Stanton, it would have been too early last Spring.'

"And as I look back upon it, I think the President was right."

It was a fitting fulfillment of the Declaration of Independence, which proclaimed that:

"All men are created equal; that they are endowed by their Creator with certain unalienable rights; that among these are life, liberty and the pursuit of happiness."

That Declaration young Abe Lincoln first read in the Gentryville constable's copy of the "Statutes of Indiana."

At noon on the first of January, 1863, William H. Seward, Secretary of State, with his son Frederick, called at the White House with the Emancipation document to be signed by the President. It was just after the regular New Year's Day reception.

Mr. Lincoln seated himself at his table, took up the pen, dipped it in the ink, held the pen a moment, then laid it down. After waiting a while he went through the same movements as before. Turning to his Secretary of State, he said, to explain his hesitation:

"I have been shaking hands since nine o'clock this morning, and my arm is almost paralyzed. If my name ever goes into history, it will be for this act, and my whole soul is in it. If my hand trembles when I sign the Proclamation, all who examine the document hereafter will say:

"'He hesitated.'"

Turning back to the table, he took the pen again and wrote, deliberately and firmly, the "Abraham Lincoln" with which the world is now familiar. Looking up at the Sewards, father and son, he smiled and said, with a sigh of relief:

"*That will do!*"

CHAPTER XIX

THE GLORY OF GETTYSBURG

THE BATTLE

The Battle of Gettysburg, which raged through July 1st, 2nd and 3d, 1863, was called the "high water mark" of the Civil War, and one of the "fifteen decisive battles" of history. It was decisive because General Robert E. Lee, with his brave army, was driven back from Gettysburg, Pennsylvania. If Lee had been victorious there, he might have destroyed Philadelphia and New York. By such a brilliant stroke he could have surrounded and captured Baltimore and Washington. This would have changed the grand result of the war.

In point of numbers, bravery and genius, the battle of Gettysburg was the greatest that had ever been fought up to that time. Glorious as this was, the greatest glory of Gettysburg lay in the experiences and utterances of one man, Abraham Lincoln, President of the United States of America.

It came at a terrible time in the progress of the war, when everything seemed to be going against the Union. There had been four disastrous defeats—twice at Bull Run, followed by Fredericksburg and Chancellorsville. Even the battle of Antietam, accounted victory enough for the President to issue his Emancipation Proclamation, proved to be a drawn battle, with terrific losses on both sides. Lee was driven back from Maryland then, it is true, but he soon won the great battles of Fredericksburg and Chancellorsville, and had made his way north into Pennsylvania.

The night after the battle of Chancellorsville (fought May 2nd and 3d, 1863), was the darkest in the history of the Civil War. President Lincoln walked the floor the whole night long, crying out in his anguish, "O what will the country say!"

To fill the decimated ranks of the army, the Government had resorted to the draft, which roused great opposition in the North and provoked foolish, unreasoning riots in New York City.

After winning the battle of Gettysburg, which the President hoped would end the war, General Meade, instead of announcing that he had captured the Confederate army, stated that he had "driven the invaders from our soil." Mr. Lincoln fell on his knees and, covering his face with his great, strong hands, cried out in tones of agony:

"'Driven the invaders from our soil!' My God, is that all?"

But Lincoln's spirits were bound to rise. Believing he was "on God's side," he felt that the cause of Right could not lose, for the Lord would save His own.

The next day, July 4th, 1863, came the surrender of Vicksburg, the stronghold of the great West. Chastened joy began to cover his gaunt and pallid features, and the light of hope shone again in his deep, gray eyes.

Calling on General Sickles, in a Washington hospital—for the general had lost a leg on the second day of the battle of Gettysburg—the President was asked why he believed that victory would be given the Federal forces at Gettysburg.

"I will tell you how it was. In the pinch of your campaign up there, when everybody seemed panic-stricken, and nobody could tell what was going to happen, I went to my room one day and locked the door, and got down on my knees before Almighty God, and prayed to him mightily for victory at Gettysburg. I told Him this was His war, and our cause His cause, but that we couldn't stand another Fredericksburg or Chancellorsville. And I then and there made a solemn vow to Almighty God that if He would stand by our boys at Gettysburg, I would stand by Him. And He *did*, and I *will!*"

The President's call on General Sickles was on the Sunday after the three-days' battle of Gettysburg, before the arrival of the gunboat at Cairo, Illinois, with the glad tidings from Vicksburg, which added new luster to the patriotic joy of Independence Day. The telegraph wires had been so generally cut on all sides of Vicksburg that the news was sent to Cairo and telegraphed to Washington. In proof that his faith even included the Mississippi blockade he went on:

"Besides, I have been praying over Vicksburg also, and believe our Heavenly Father is going to give us victory there, too, because we need it, in order to bisect the Confederacy, and let 'the Father of Waters flow unvexed to the sea.'"

THE ADDRESS

Not long after the conflict at Gettysburg a movement was on foot to devote a large part of that battle-ground to a national cemetery.

The Hon. Edward Everett, prominent in national and educational affairs, and the greatest living orator, was invited to deliver the grand oration. The President was asked, if he could, to come and make a few dedicatory remarks, but Mr. Everett was to be the chief speaker of the occasion.

The Sunday before the 19th of November, 1863, the date of the dedication, the President went with his friend Noah Brooks to Gardner's gallery, in Washington, where he had promised to sit for his photograph. While there he showed Mr. Brooks a proof of Everett's oration which had been sent to him. As this printed address covered two newspaper pages, Mr. Lincoln struck an attitude and quoted from a speech by Daniel Webster:

"Solid men of Boston, make no long orations!" and burst out laughing. When Mr. Brooks asked about *his* speech for that occasion, Mr. Lincoln replied: "I've got it written, but not licked into shape yet. It's short, *short*, SHORT!"

During the forenoon of the 18th, Secretary John Hay was anxious lest the President be late for the special Presidential train, which was to leave at noon for Gettysburg.

"Don't worry, John," said Mr. Lincoln. "I'm like the man who was going to be hung, and saw the crowds pushing and hurrying past the cart in which he was being taken to the place of execution. He called out to them: 'Don't hurry, boys. There won't be anything going on till I get there!'"

When the train stopped, on the way to Gettysburg, a little girl on the platform held up a bouquet to Mr. Lincoln, lisping: "Flowerth for the Prethident."

He reached out, took her up and kissed her, saying:

"You're a sweet little rosebud yourself. I hope your life will open into perpetual beauty and goodness."

About noon on the 19th of November, the distinguished party arrived in a procession and took seats on the platform erected for the exercises. The President was seated in a rocking-chair placed there for him. There were fifteen thousand people waiting, some of whom had been standing in the sun for hours. It was a warm day and a Quaker woman near the platform fainted. An alarm was given and the unconscious woman was in danger of being crushed.

The President sprang to the edge of the staging and called out:

"Here, let me get hold of that lady."

With a firm, strong grasp he extricated her from the crush and seated her in his rocking-chair. When that modest woman "came to," she saw fifteen thousand pairs of eyes watching her while the President of the United States was fanning her tenderly.

This was too much for her. She gasped:

"I feel—better—now. I want to go—back to—my husband!"

"Now, my dear lady," said Mr. Lincoln. "You are all right here. I had an awful time pulling you up out of there, and I couldn't stick you back again!"

A youth who stood near the platform in front of the President says that, while Mr. Everett was orating, Mr. Lincoln took his "little speech," as he called it, out of his pocket, and conned it over like a schoolboy with a half-learned lesson. The President had put the finishing touches on it that morning. As it was expected that the President would make a few offhand remarks, no one seems to have noticed its simple grandeur until it was printed in the newspapers.

Yet Mr. Lincoln was interrupted four or five times during the two minutes by applause. The fact that the President was speaking was sufficient, no matter what he said. The people would have applauded Abraham Lincoln if he had merely recited the multiplication table! When he finished, they gave "three times three cheers" for the President of the United States, and three cheers for each of the State Governors present.

That afternoon there was a patriotic service in one of the churches which the President decided to attend. Taking Secretary Seward with him, he called on an old cobbler named John Burns, of whose courage in the battle of Gettysburg Mr. Lincoln had just heard. Those who planned the dedication did not think the poor cobbler was of much account. The old hero, now known through Bret Harte's poem, "John Burns of Gettysburg," had the pride and joy of having all the village and visitors see him march to the church between President Lincoln and Secretary Seward. This simple act was "just like Lincoln!" He honored Gettysburg in thus honoring one of its humblest citizens. It was Abraham Lincoln's tribute to the patriotism of the dear "common people" whom he said "God must love."

CHAPTER XX

"NO END OF A BOY"

"The Story of Young Abraham Lincoln" would be incomplete without some insight into the perfect boyishness of the President of the United States. When the cares of State and the horrors of war had made his homely yet beautiful face pallid and seamed, till it became a sensitive map of the Civil War, it was said that the only times the President was ever happy were when he was playing with little Tad.

He used to carry the boy on his shoulder or "pick-a-back," cantering through the spacious rooms of the Executive Mansion, both yelling like Comanches. The little boy was lonely after Willie died, and the father's heart yearned over the only boy left at home, for Robert was at Harvard until near the close of the war, when he went to the front as an aide to General Grant. So little Tad was his father's most constant companion and the President became the boy's only playfellow. Mr. Lincoln, with a heart as full of faith as a little child's, had always lived in deep sympathy with the children, and this feeling was intensified toward his own offspring.

When Abe Lincoln was living in New Salem he distinguished himself by caring for the little children—a thing beneath the dignity of the other young men of the settlement.

Hannah Armstrong, wife of the Clary's Grove bully, whom Abe had to "lick" to a finish in order to establish himself on a solid basis in New Salem society, told how friendly their relations became after the thrashing he gave her husband:

"Abe would come to our house, drink milk, eat mush, cornbread and butter, bring the children candy and rock the cradle." (This seemed a strange thing to her.) "He would nurse babies—do anything to accommodate anybody."

HOW HE REPAID THE ARMSTRONGS' KINDNESS

The Armstrong baby, Willie, grew to be a youth of wrong habits, and was nicknamed "Duff." He was drawn, one afternoon, into a bad quarrel with another rough young man, named Metzker, who was brutally beaten. In the evening a vicious young man, named Morris, joined the row and the lad was struck on the head and died without telling who had dealt the fatal blow. The blame was thrown upon "Duff" Armstrong, who was arrested. Illinois law preventing him from testifying in his own behalf.

When Lawyer Lincoln heard of the case, he wrote as follows:

"SPRINGFIELD, ILL., September, 1857.

"DEAR MRS. ARMSTRONG:

"I have just heard of your deep affliction, and the arrest of your son for murder.

"I can hardly believe that he can be capable of the crime alleged against him.

"It does not seem possible. I am anxious that he should be given a fair trial, at any rate; and gratitude for your long-continued kindness to me in adverse circumstances prompts me to offer my humble services gratuitously in his behalf.

"It will afford me an opportunity to requite, in a small degree, the favors I received at your hand, and that of your lamented husband, when your roof afforded me a grateful shelter, without money and without price.

"Yours truly,
"A. LINCOLN."

The feeling in the neighborhood where the crime was committed was so intense that it was decided that it must be taken over to the next county to secure a fair trial. Lawyer Lincoln was on hand to defend the son of his old friend.

Besides those who testified to the bad character of the young prisoner, one witness, named Allen, testified that he saw "Duff" Armstrong strike the blow which killed Metzker.

"Couldn't you be mistaken about this?" asked Mr. Lincoln. "What time did you see it?"

"Between nine and ten o'clock that night."

"Are you certain that you saw the prisoner strike the blow?—Be careful—remember—you are under oath!"

"I am sure. There is no doubt about it."

"But wasn't it dark at that hour?"

"No, the moon was shining bright."

"Then you say there was a moon and it was not dark."

"Yes, it was light enough for me to see him hit Metzker on the head."

"Now I want you to be very careful. I understand you to say the murder was committed about half past nine o'clock, and there was a bright moon at the time?"

"Yes, sir," said the witness positively.

"Very well. That is all."

Then Lawyer Lincoln produced an almanac showing that there was no moon that night till the early hours of the morning.

"This witness has perjured himself," he said, "and his whole story is a lie."

"Duff" Armstrong was promptly acquitted. The tears of that widowed mother and the gratitude of the boy he had rocked were the best sort of pay to Lawyer Lincoln for an act of kindness and life-saving.

"JUST WHAT'S THE MATTER WITH THE WHOLE WORLD!"

A Springfield neighbor used to say that it was almost a habit with Mr. Lincoln to carry his children about on his shoulders. Indeed, the man said he seldom saw the tall lawyer go by without one or both boys perched on high or tugging at the tails of his long coat. This neighbor relates that he was attracted to the door of his own house one day by a great noise of crying children, and saw Mr. Lincoln passing with the two boys in their usual position, and both were howling lustily.

"Why, Mr. Lincoln, what's the matter?" he asked in astonishment.

"Just what's the matter with the whole world," the lawyer replied coolly. "I've got three walnuts, and each wants two."

THE "BUCKING" CHESS BOARD

Several years later Judge Treat, of Springfield was playing chess with Mr. Lincoln in his law office when Tad came in to call his father to supper. The boy, impatient at the delay of the slow and silent game, tried to break it up by a flank movement against the chess board, but the attacks were warded off, each time, by his father's long arms.

The child disappeared, and when the two players had begun to believe they were to be permitted to end the game in peace, the table suddenly "bucked" and the board and chessmen were sent flying all over the floor.

Judge Treat was much vexed, and expressed impatience, not hesitating to tell Mr. Lincoln that the boy ought to be punished severely.

Mr. Lincoln replied, as he gently took down his hat to go home to supper:

"Considering the position of your pieces, judge, at the time of the upheaval, I think you have no reason to complain."

WHEN TAD GOT A SPANKING

Yet, indulgent as he was, there were some things Mr. Lincoln would not allow even his youngest child to do. An observer who saw the President-elect and his family in their train on the way to Washington to take the helm of State, relates that little Tad amused himself by raising the car window an inch or two and trying, by shutting it down suddenly, to catch the fingers of the curious boys outside who were holding themselves up by their hands on the window sill of the car to catch sight of the new President and his family.

The President-elect, who had to go out to the platform to make a little speech to a crowd at nearly every stop, noticed Tad's attempts to pinch the boys' fingers. He spoke sharply to his son and commanded him to stop that. Tad obeyed for a time, but his father, catching him at the same trick again, leaned over, and taking the little fellow across his knee, gave him a good, sound spanking, exclaiming as he did so:

"Why do you want to mash those boys' fingers?"

THE TRUE STORY OF BOB'S LOSING THE INAUGURAL ADDRESS

Mr. Lincoln was always lenient when the offense was against himself. The Hon. Robert Todd Lincoln, the only living son of the great President, tells how the satchel containing his father's inaugural address was lost for a time. Some writers have related the story of this loss, stating that it all happened at Harrisburg, and telling how the President-elect discovered a bag like his own, and on opening it found only a pack of greasy cards, a bottle of whisky and a soiled paper collar. Also that Mr. Lincoln was "reminded" of a cheap, ill-fitting story—but none of these things really took place.

Here is the true story, as related to the writer by Robert Lincoln himself:

"My father had confided to me the care of the satchel containing his inaugural address. It was lost for a little while during the stay of our party at the old Bates House in Indianapolis. When we entered the hotel I set the bag down with the other luggage, which was all removed to a room back of the clerk's desk.

"As soon as I missed the valise I went right to father, in great distress of mind. He ordered a search made. We were naturally much alarmed, for it was the only copy he had of his inaugural address, which he had carefully written before leaving Springfield. Of course, he added certain parts after reaching Washington. The missing bag was soon found in a safe place.

"Instead of taking out the precious manuscript and stuffing it into his own pocket, father handed it right back to me, saying:

"'There, Bob, see if you can't take better care of it this time'—and you may be sure I was true to the trust he placed in me. Why, I hardly let that precious gripsack get out of my sight during my waking hours all the rest of the long roundabout journey to Washington."

THE TERRIBLE LONELINESS AFTER WILLIE DIED

The death of Willie, who was nearly three years older than Tad, early in 1862, during their first year in the White House, nearly broke his father's heart. It was said that Mr. Lincoln never recovered from that bereavement. It made him yearn the more tenderly over his youngest son who sadly missed the brother who had been his constant companion.

It was natural for a lad who was so much indulged to take advantage of his freedom. Tad had a slight impediment in his speech which made the street urchins laugh at him, and even cabinet members, because they could not understand him, considered him a little nuisance. So Tad, though known as "the child of the nation," and greatly beloved and petted by those who knew him for a lovable affectionate child, found himself alone in a class by himself, and against all classes of people.

TURNING THE HOSE ON HIGH OFFICIALS

He illustrated this spirit one day by getting hold of the hose and turning it on some dignified State officials, several army officers, and finally on a soldier on guard who was ordered to charge and take possession of that water battery. Although that little escapade appealed to the President's sense of humor, for he himself liked nothing better than to take generals and pompous officials down "a peg or two," Tad got well spanked for the havoc he wrought that day.

BREAKING INTO A CABINET MEETING

The members of the President's cabinet had reason to be annoyed by the boy's frequent interruptions. He seemed to have the right of way wherever his father happened to be. No matter if Senator Sumner or Secretary Stanton was discussing some weighty matter of State or war, if Tad came in, his father turned from the men of high estate to minister to the wants of his little boy. He did it to get rid of him, for of course he knew Tad would raise such a racket that no one could talk or think till *his* wants were disposed of.

AN EXECUTIVE ORDER ON THE COMMISSARY DEPARTMENT FOR TAD AND HIS BOY FRIENDS

A story is told of the boy's interruption of a council of war. This habit of Tad's enraged Secretary Stanton, whose horror of the boy was similar to that of an elephant for a mouse. The President was giving his opinion on a certain piece of strategy which he thought the general in question might carry out—when a great noise was heard out in the hall, followed by a number of sharp raps on the door of the cabinet room.

Strategy, war, everything was, for the moment forgotten by the President, whose wan face assumed an expression of unusual pleasure, while he gathered up his great, weary length from different parts of the room as he had half lain, sprawling about, across and around his chair and the great table.

"That's Tad," he exclaimed, "I wonder what that boy wants now." On his way to open the door, Mr. Lincoln explained that those knocks had just been adopted by the boy and himself, as part of the telegraph system, and that he was obliged to let the lad in—"for it wouldn't do to go back on the code now," he added, half in apology for permitting such a sudden break in their deliberations.

When the door was opened, Tad, with flushed face and sparkling eyes, sprang in and threw his arms around his father's neck. The President straightened up and embraced the boy with an expression of happiness never seen on his face except while playing with his little son.

Mr. Lincoln turned, with the boy still in his arms, to explain that he and Tad had agreed upon this telegraphic code to prevent the lad from bursting in upon them without warning. The members of the cabinet looked puzzled or disgusted, as though they failed to see that several startling raps could be any better than having Tad break in with a whoop or a wail, as had been the boy's custom.

ISSUING THE EXECUTIVE ORDER ON PETER FOR PIE

The boy raised a question of right. He had besieged Peter, the colored steward, demanding that a dinner be served to several urchins he had picked up outside—two of whom were sons of soldiers. Peter had protested that he "had other fish to fry" just then.

The President recognized at once that this was a case for diplomacy. Turning to various members of the cabinet, he called on each to contribute from his store of wisdom, what would be best to do in a case of such vast importance. Tad looked on in wonder as his father set the great machinery of government in motion to make out a commissary order on black Peter, which would force that astonished servant to deliver certain pieces of pie and other desired eatables to Tad, for himself and his boy friends.

At last an "order" was prepared by the Chief Executive of the United States directing "The Commissary Department of the Presidential Residence to issue rations to Lieutenant Tad Lincoln and his five associates, two of whom are the sons of soldiers in the Army of the Potomac."

With an expression of deep gravity and a solemn flourish, the President tendered this Commissary Order to the lieutenant, his son, saying as he presented the document:

"I reckon Peter will *have* to come to time now."

CHAPTER XXI

LIEUTENANT TAD LINCOLN, PATRIOT

There was no more sturdy little patriot in the whole country than Lieutenant Tad Lincoln, "the child of the nation," nor had the President of the United States a more devoted admirer and follower than his own small son. A word from his father would melt the lad to tears and submission, or bring him out of a nervous tantrum with his small round face wreathed with smiles, and a chuckling in his throat of "Papa-day, my papa-day!" No one knew exactly what the boy meant by papa-day. It was his pet name for the dearest man on earth, and it was his only way of expressing the greatest pleasure his boyish heart was able to hold. It was the "sweetest word ever heard" by the war-burdened, crushed and sorrowing soul of the broken-hearted President of the United States.

Mr. Lincoln took his youngest son with him everywhere—on his great mission to Fortress Monroe, and they—"the long and the short of it," the soldiers said—marched hand in hand through the streets of fallen Richmond. The understanding between the man and the boy was so complete and sacred, that some acts which seemed to outsiders absurd and ill-fitting, became perfectly right and proper when certain unknown facts were taken into account.

WAVING THE "STARS AND BARS" OUT OF A WHITE HOUSE WINDOW

For instance, one night, during an enthusiastic serenade at the White House, after a great victory of the northern armies, when the President had been out and made a happy speech in response to the congratulations he had received, everybody was horrified to see the Confederate "Stars and Bars" waving frantically from an upper window with shouts followed by shrieks as old Edward, the faithful colored servant, pulled in the flag and the boy who was guilty of the mischief.

"That was little Tad!" exclaimed some one in the crowd. Many laughed, but some spectators thought the boy ought to be punished for such a treasonable outbreak on the part of a President's boy in a soldier's uniform.

"If he don't know any better than that," said one man, "he should be taught better. It's an insult to the North and the President ought to stop it and apologize, too."

"BOYS IN BLUE" AND "BOYS IN GRAY"

But little Tad understood his father's spirit better than the crowd did. He knew that the President's love was not confined to "the Boys in Blue," but that his heart went out also to "the Boys in Gray." The soldiers were all "boys" to him. They knew he loved them. They said among themselves: "He cares for us. He takes our part. We will fight for him; yes, we will die for him."

And a large part of the common soldier's patriotism was this heart-response of "the boys" to the great "boy" in the White House. That was the meaning of their song as they trooped to the front at his call:

"We are coming, Father Abraham;
Three hundred thousand more."

Little Tad saw plenty of evidences of his father's love for the younger soldiers—the real boys of the army. Going always with the President, he had heard his "Papa-day" say of several youths condemned to be shot for sleeping at their post or some like offense:

"That boy is worth more above ground than under;" or, "A live boy can serve his country better than a dead one."

"Give the boys a chance," was Abraham Lincoln's motto. He hadn't had much of a chance himself and he wanted all other boys to have a fair show. His own father had been too hard with him, and he was going to make it up to all the other boys he could reach. This passion for doing good to others began in the log cabin when he had no idea he could ever be exercising his loving kindness in the Executive Mansion—the Home of the Nation. "With malice toward none, with charity for all," was the rule of his life in the backwoods as well as in the National Capital.

And "the Boys in Gray" were his "boys," too, but they didn't understand, so they had wandered away—they were a little wayward, but he would win them back. The great chivalrous South has learned, since those bitter, ruinous days, that Abraham Lincoln was the best friend the South then had in the North. Tad had seen his father show great tenderness to all the "boys" he met in the gray uniform, but the President had few opportunities to show his tenderness to the South—though there was a secret pigeonhole in his desk stuffed full of threats of assassination. He was not afraid of death—indeed, he was glad to die if it would do his "boys" and the country any good. But it hurt him deep in his heart to know that some of his beloved children misunderstood him so that they were willing to kill him!

It was no one's bullet which made Abraham Lincoln a martyr. All his life he had shown the spirit of love which was willing to give his very life if it could save or help others.

All these things little Tad could not have explained, but they were inbred into the deep understanding of the big father and the small son who were living in the White House as boys together.

MR. LINCOLN'S LAST SPEECH AND HOW TAD HELPED

A few days after the war ended at Appomattox, a great crowd came to the White House to serenade the President. It was Tuesday evening, April 11, 1865. Mr. Lincoln had written a short address for the occasion. The times were so out of joint and every word was so important that the President could not trust himself to speak off-hand.

A friend stepped out on the northern portico with him to hold the candle by which Mr. Lincoln was to read his speech. Little Tad was with his father, as usual, and when the President had finished reading a page of his manuscript he let it flutter down, like a leaf, or a big white butterfly, for Tad to catch. When the pages came too slowly the boy pulled his father's coat-tail, piping up in a muffled, excited tone:

"Give me 'nother paper, Papa-day."

To the few in the front of the crowd who witnessed this little by-play it seemed ridiculous that the President of the United States should allow any child to behave like that and hamper him while delivering a great address which would wield a national, if not world-wide influence. But little Tad did not trouble his father in the least. It was a part of the little game they were constantly playing together.

The address opened with these words:

"FELLOW-CITIZENS: We meet this evening not in sorrow, but gladness of heart. The evacuation of Petersburg and Richmond, and the surrender of the principal insurgent army (at Appomattox) give hope of a righteous and speedy peace whose joyous expression cannot be restrained. In the midst of this, however, He from whom all blessings flow must not be forgotten. A call for national thanksgiving is being prepared and will be duly promulgated."

"GIVE US 'DIXIE,' BOYS!"

Then he went on outlining a policy of peace and friendship toward the South—showing a spirit far higher and more advanced than that of the listening crowd. On concluding his address and bidding the assembled multitude good night, he turned to the serenading band and shouted joyously:

"Give us 'Dixie,' boys; play 'Dixie.' We have a right to that tune now."

There was a moment of silence. Some of the people gasped, as they had done when they saw Tad waving the Confederate flag at the window. But the band, loyal even to a mere whim (as they then thought it) of "Father Abraham," started the long-forbidden tune, and the President, bowing, retired, with little Tad, within the White House. Those words, "Give us 'Dixie,' boys," were President Lincoln's last public utterance.

As Mr. Lincoln came in through the door after speaking to the crowd, Mrs. Lincoln—who had been, with a group of friends, looking on from within—exclaimed to him:

"You must not be so careless. Some one could easily have shot you while you were speaking there—and you know they are threatening your life!"

The President smiled at his wife, through a look of inexpressible pain and sadness, and shrugged his great shoulders, but "still he answered not a word."

THE SEPARATION OF THE TWO "BOYS"

At a late hour Good Friday night, that same week, little Tad came in alone at a basement door of the White House from the National Theater, where he knew the manager, and some of the company, had made a great pet of him. He had often gone there alone or with his tutor. How he had heard the terrible news from Ford's Theater is not known, but he came up the lower stairway with heartrending cries like a wounded animal. Seeing Thomas Pendel, the faithful doorkeeper, he wailed from his breaking heart:

"Tom Pen, Tom Pen, they have killed Papa-day! They have killed my Papa-day!"

After the funeral the little fellow was more lonely than ever. It was hard to have his pony burned up in the stable. It was harder still to lose Brother Willie, his constant companion, and now his mother was desperately ill, and his father had been killed. Tad, of course, could not comprehend why any one could be so cruel and wicked as to wish to murder his darling Papa-day, who loved every one so!

He wandered through the empty rooms, aching with loneliness, murmuring softly to himself:

"Papa-day, where's my Papa-day. I'm tired—tired of playing alone. I want to play together. Please, Papa-day, come back and play with your little Tad."

Young though he was he could not sleep long at night. His sense of loneliness penetrated his dreams. Sometimes he would chuckle and gurgle in an ecstacy, as he had done when riding on his father's back, romping through the stately rooms. He would throw his arm about the neck of the doorkeeper or lifeguard who had lain down beside him to console the boy and try to get him to sleep. When the man spoke to comfort him, Tad would find out his terrible mistake, that his father was not with him.

Then he would wail again in the bitterness of his disappointment:

"Papa-day, where's my Papa-day?"

"Your papa's gone 'way off"—said his companion, his voice breaking with emotion—"gone to heaven."

Tad opened his eyes wide with wonder. "Is Papa-day happy in heaven?" he asked eagerly.

"Yes, yes, I'm sure he's happy there, Taddie dear; now go to sleep."

"Papa-day's happy. I'm glad—*so* glad!"—sighed the little boy—"for Papa-day never was happy here."

Then he fell into his first sweet sleep since that terrible night.

GIVE THE BOYS A CHANCE"

The fond-hearted little fellow went abroad with his mother a few years after the tragedy that broke both their lives. By a surgical operation, and by struggling manfully, he had corrected the imperfection in his speech. But the heart of little Tad had been broken. While still a lad he joined his fond father in the Beyond.

"Give the boys a chance," had amounted to a passion with Abraham Lincoln, yet through great wickedness and sad misunderstandings his own little son was robbed of this great boon. Little Tad had been denied the one chance he sorely needed for his very existence. For this, as for all the inequities the great heart of the White House was prepared. His spirit had shone through his whole life as if in letters of living fire:

"With malice toward none; with charity for all."

Milton Keynes UK
Ingram Content Group UK Ltd.
UKHW030909151124
451262UK00006B/878